TURNING POINTS

By Jennifer Lombardo

THE TRAIL OF TEARS

Cavendish Square
New York

Published in 2021 by Cavendish Square Publishing, LLC
243 5th Avenue, Suite 136, New York, NY 10016

First Edition

Portions of this work were originally authored by Lydia Bjornlund and published as *The Trail of Tears: The Relocation of the Cherokee Nation* (*American History*). All new material this edition authored by Jennifer Lombardo.

Library of Congress Cataloging-in-Publication Data
Names: Lombardo, Jennifer, author.
Title: The Trail of Tears / Jennifer Lombardo.
Description: First edition. | New York : Cavendish Square Publishing, [2021] | Series: Turning points | Includes bibliographical references and index.
Identifiers: LCCN 2019049001 (print) | LCCN 2019049002 (ebook) | ISBN 9781502657756 (library binding) | ISBN 9781502657749 (paperback) | ISBN 9781502657763 (ebook)
Subjects: LCSH: Trail of Tears, 1838-1839–Juvenile literature. | Cherokee Indians–Relocation–Juvenile literature. | Indian Territory–History–Juvenile literature. | Southern States–History–Juvenile literature.
Classification: LCC E99.C5 L64 2021 (print) | LCC E99.C5 (ebook) | DDC 973.5/7–dc23
LC record available at https://lccn.loc.gov/2019049001
LC ebook record available at https://lccn.loc.gov/2019049002

Editor: Jennifer Lombardo
Copy Editor: Michelle Denton
Designer: Deanna Paternostro

Printed in the United States of America

TABLE OF CONTENTS

INTRODUCTION

A HISTORY OF SUFFERING

Ever since the first white Europeans arrived in what is now the United States, there has been conflict between them and the people who first inhabited North America. In the past, it was the Native Americans who received most of the blame; they were often depicted as bloodthirsty savages who would attack people for no reason. However, a better understanding of historical events has revealed that it was most frequently the white settlers and leaders who were the aggressors.

All native groups suffered in various ways after the Europeans invaded North America, but the story of the Trail of Tears stands out as a particularly horrifying incident. In the 1830s, the native groups that lived in the Southeast—including the Cherokee, Creek, Chickasaw, Choctaw, and Seminole nations—were forced from their homes and sent to government camps, where they awaited their departure to land that had been set aside for them in present-day Oklahoma. The US government had decided to stop trying to get them to move west of the Mississippi River by legal and political means and decided to take more direct action instead, physically forcing them to relocate. This final, brutal removal of the Native Americans from their ancestral lands has become known as the Trail of Tears.

Before the US government took control of their land, Native Americans could travel when and where they chose.

An Act of Greed

In the 1830s, about 100,000 Native Americans were forced to leave their homes and make a dangerous journey to reservations in the West. The Cherokee are the main group people associate with the Trail of Tears, but many historians include the Creek, Chickasaw, Choctaw, and Seminole nations in their accounts of the Trail of Tears. Other Native Americans living in other parts of the growing United States experienced their own tearful trails as they, too, were forced from their homelands. According to the *Encyclopedia Britannica*, "The term Trail of Tears invokes the collective suffering those people experienced, although it is most commonly used in reference to the removal experiences of the Southeast Indians generally and the Cherokee nation specifically."[1]

By the 1820s, an increasing number of white settlers were living illegally on land owned by the Cherokee Nation—a trend made

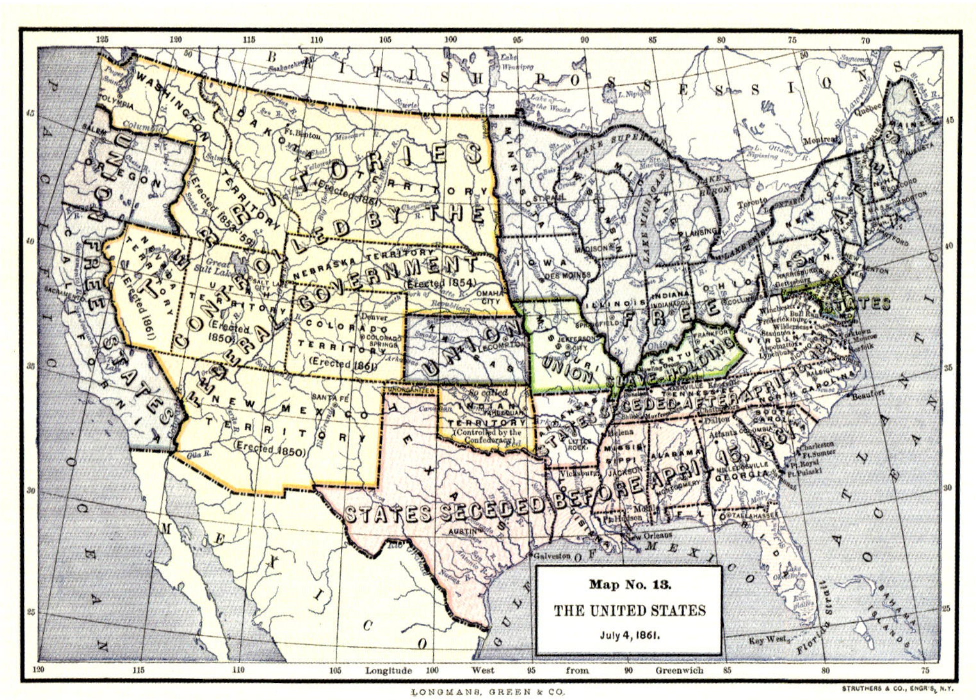

This map shows present-day Oklahoma labeled as Indian Territory. In 1907, when Oklahoma became a state, Indian Territory ceased to exist.

worse after gold was discovered on Cherokee land in 1828. State governments ignored the Cherokee's petition for help to remove the illegal settlers. In fact, most states responded by putting additional pressure on the Cherokee to leave. The passage of the Indian Removal Act in 1830 made it a federal issue. This act, pushed through Congress by President Andrew Jackson, set aside land in so-called "Indian Territory" (present-day Oklahoma) for Native Americans in exchange for their land in the East. The law required all Native Americans to move west of the Mississippi River within a few years of its passage. By 1838, most native groups in the Southeast other than the Cherokee Nation had chosen to leave or had already been forced to relocate.

Still, the Cherokee refused to believe the US government would ignore its promises and treaties. They pointed to past agreements that had been signed in good faith that they believed gave them the right to their homelands. Cherokee delegations went to Washington, DC, to plead their case before Congress. They met with US presidents and cabinet members to request exemption from the Indian Removal Act; they took their case all the way to the Supreme Court. For years, the Cherokee believed that justice would prevail.

Betrayal of Trust

The Cherokee's faith in the US government proved unfounded. In 1838, the US Army was ordered to evacuate all Cherokee people from their homeland and lead them westward to their new land in Indian Territory. They were forced from their homes and moved into hastily constructed forts. Crowded together in unsanitary conditions, the Native Americans became susceptible to diseases that swept through the forts. Hundreds died before they even started their westward journey.

To get to the land set aside for them, men, women, and children walked 800 to 1,000 miles (1,288 to 1,609 kilometers)—a journey that took up to 6 months. The native people suffered greatly along the way. Boats capsized. Wagons broke down. Food was scarce and spoiled. Death was common. Some turned back, but most had no choice but to continue on, desperately hoping to reach their destination. In one group, only 489 of an estimated 800 who set out together arrived in Indian Territory. One white volunteer from Georgia who took part in the removal later wrote, "I fought through the Civil War and have seen men shot to pieces and slaughtered by thousands, but the Cherokee removal was the cruelest work I ever knew."[2]

Of the 100,000 Native Americans who were removed, an estimated 15,000 died. This gruesome death percentage was even worse among the Cherokee, specifically. Historians estimate that at least 4,000 of the 16,000 Cherokee who were living in the southeastern United States lost their lives during the journey.

Some scholars, however, believe that the impact was much greater, particularly when taking into account the number of children who would have been born during the late 1830s had removal not occurred. One scholar who undertook an analysis of the Cherokee population figures concluded that "a total mortality figure of 8,000 for the Trail of Tears period, twice the supposed 4,000, may not be at all unreasonable."[3] Because of this tragic loss of life, the Cherokee today still call the routes they took westward *nuna dat shun'yi*, which means "the place where they cried."

Following a Precedent

The United States is not unique in its treatment of indigenous, or native, people. Throughout history and around the world, more powerful groups have frequently pushed people off their land. In some places, indigenous people have been assimilated into the new culture, often as slaves or laborers. In others, they have been wiped out entirely, intentionally by war or unintentionally through disease and famine. Sometimes, they have been forced to move. Since their first contact with European settlers, Native Americans have been subjected to all three. Even today, in some parts of the world, people are forced to flee to safer areas because someone more powerful wants their land or its resources. Also common today are disagreements between two different cultures—two different ways of life—that result in ongoing conflict.

Strictly defined, the Trail of Tears describes the main routes that the Cherokee and other tribes took from the Southeast to the land the US government identified as their new home in Indian Territory. However, the Trail of Tears is not just a series of routes. It has come to mean the journey itself—the experience of a people. The term defines the forced movement of a people and the immense sadness they felt. The Trail of Tears represents a terrible time in history caused by prejudice, greed, and the entitlement felt by the white citizens of the growing United States.

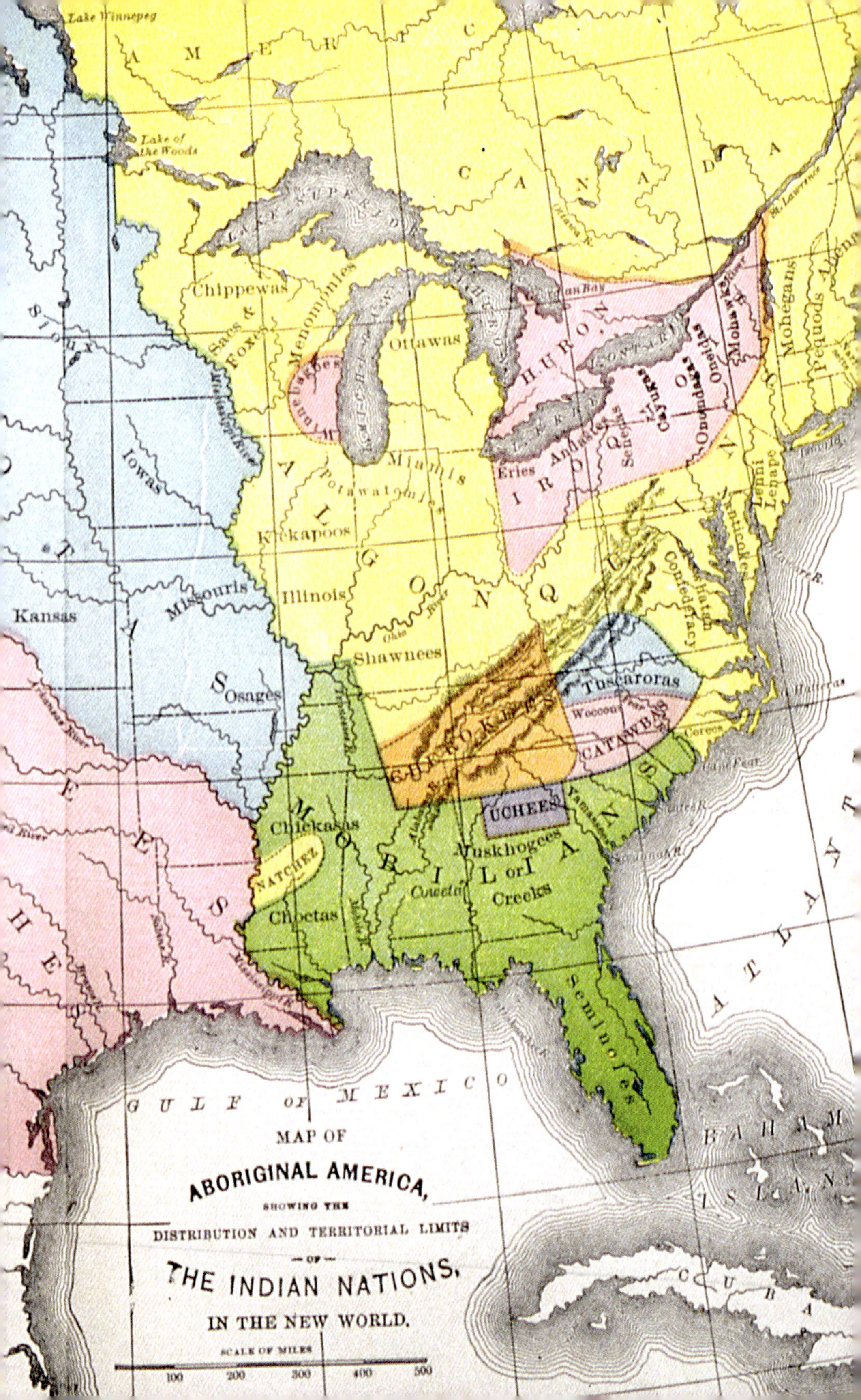
MAP OF
ABORIGINAL AMERICA,
SHOWING THE
DISTRIBUTION AND TERRITORIAL LIMITS
OF
THE INDIAN NATIONS,
IN THE NEW WORLD.
SCALE OF MILES
100 200 300 400 500
Lake Winnepeg
Lake of the Woods
C A N A D A
Chippewas
Sacs & Foxes
Menomonies
Ottawas
HURON
Eries
IROQUOIS
Senecas
Cayugas
Onondagas
Oneidas
Mohawks
Mohegans
Pequods
Lenni Lenape
Miamis
Potawatomies
Kickapoos
Illinois
Shawnees
ALGONQUIN
Sioux
Iowas
Missouris
Kansas
Osages
Tuscaroras
Woccons
CATAWBAS
CHEROKEES
UCHEES
Chickasas
NATCHEZ
Choctas
MOBILIANS
Muskhogees or Creeks
Coweta
Seminoles
Corees
GULF OF MEXICO
ATLANTIC
BAHAMA ISLANDS
CUBA

CHAPTER ONE

LIFE BEFORE AND DURING COLONIZATION

The history of what eventually became the United States often focuses on the original 13 British colonies, but Europeans had been conducting their own explorations of North America since the 1500s. It's commonly stated that Christopher Columbus was the first to land in America in 1492, but he didn't land in what's now the United States. As far as historians can tell, the first contact between Europeans and native groups in North America occurred in 1540, when Spanish explorer Hernando de Soto met a group of Cherokee while leading an expedition in search of gold in present-day Georgia and South Carolina.

The Cherokee had lived in southeastern North America for generations before the Spanish and other European explorers arrived. Their lands spread across parts of the modern states of Georgia, Tennessee, North Carolina, South Carolina, and Alabama, covering about 140,000 square miles (362,600 sq km). At their peak, the Cherokee were the largest and most powerful tribe in southeastern North America.

When the Cherokee began their relationships with European explorers and settlers, they were living in well-established villages with a sophisticated culture. Though they looked different to these newcomers, the Cherokee, like other native groups of North

This map shows where different Native American groups lived in what's now the United States before their lands were taken over by settlers.

America, had homes, families, and customs that were important to their daily life. They wanted to protect and care for their traditions the best they could.

Domestic Life

"Cherokee" comes from a Creek word, *Chelokee*, meaning "people of a different speech." Most Cherokee called themselves *Aniyunwiya*, which means "the principal people," or *Keetoowah*, which means "people of Kituwa," referencing the original village of the Cherokee.

The early Cherokee lived in many villages. Most villages consisted of about 50 families. Each village had a council house—a building where meetings were held. It was a circular structure with thick mud walls. The council house had to be large enough to hold several

In summer, Cherokee lived in wattle and daub houses similar to this one.

hundred people because the entire village met there for ceremonies or to discuss important issues.

The early Cherokee had two types of houses. Large, rectangular houses with wooden sides and roofs were built for the summer months. The wooden sides would be covered in clay; this style of building is called wattle and daub. Most houses were quite large to allow for many family members to live together. Small, round houses called *asi* were used in the winter. Each one had a framework of large poles interwoven with branches and walls filled in with thick mud. At the center of the *asi* was a fire pit that provided warmth. In addition to these houses, Cherokee family homesteads included outbuildings to store corn and other crops to last through the winter.

The family was the core of Cherokee life. Extended family members—grandparents, aunts, uncles, and cousins—lived in the same village, and often in the same house, until separated by marriage. Cherokee families were divided into seven clans, which were essentially larger groups of more distant relatives. The Cherokee clans were called Bird, Blue, Deer, Long Hair, Paint, Wild Potato, and Wolf.

Historically, the Cherokee were a matrilineal people, which means each person traced their family background through their mother's family. At birth, a Cherokee baby became a member of their mother's clan. The clan served as an extended family. A Cherokee traveling far from home could expect to receive food and shelter from members of their clan in other villages.

If a Cherokee woman married a white settler, her children were considered Cherokee, and they became part of her clan. As intermarriages became more common, the Cherokee Nation passed a law giving Cherokee citizenship to the children of white women married to Cherokee. As a result, by the time of the Trail of Tears, the Cherokee Nation included hundreds of descendants of white settlers in their numbers. In some communities, Cherokee who were of mixed race outnumbered those with only Cherokee ancestry.

It did not matter how many white ancestors a Cherokee had; anyone with Cherokee blood was a Cherokee in the eyes of both the Cherokee and the US government. Mixed-race Cherokee lived

PAST MEETS PRESENT: CLAIMING TO BE CHEROKEE

Today, the actual number of people with Cherokee blood is somewhat obscured because so many people claim to be at least part Cherokee when they have no Cherokee in their family tree. In fact, according to the website *Slate*, more people claim to be descended from Cherokee than from any other Native American group. Partially, this is due to the fact that Cherokee clans tended to be more open to intermarriage than other Native American groups. After they were relocated, the Cherokee's high literacy rate and their ties to white people allowed them to travel far more extensively than people from other Native American groups, allowing even more intermarriage to take place.

However, another reason for the high number of unproven claims of even tiny amounts of Cherokee blood is that, after the Trail of Tears and the American Civil War, the Cherokee began to be viewed more idealistically. Instead of being seen as a problem to be dealt with, the way the federal government had, people began to see them as freedom fighters. This was especially true in the South, where, not coincidentally, members of the recently defeated Confederate army were also viewed as freedom fighters. According to *Slate*, "Throughout the South in the 1840s and 1850s, large numbers of whites began claiming they were descended from a Cherokee great-grandmother."[1] Many also claimed their great-grandmother had been a princess, despite the fact that the Cherokee did not have a system of royalty; this was because, in the South, a strong emphasis was placed on heritage as a marker of social status. These stories were then told to their descendants, who believed they were true and, in fact, had good reason not to investigate the claims. As *Slate* noted, "Shifting one's identity to claim ownership of an imagined Cherokee past is at once a way to authenticate your American-ness and absolve yourself of complicity [participation] in the crimes Americans committed against the tribe across history."[2] Of course, this does not mean that everyone who says they have Cherokee ancestry is lying, but it is worth noting that there are likely fewer Cherokee than the US census says there are.

1. Gregory D. Smithers, "Why Do So Many Americans Think They Have Cherokee Blood?," *Slate*, October 1, 2015, slate.com/news-and-politics/2015/10/cherokee-blood-why-do-so-many-americans-believe-they-have-cherokee-ancestry.html.

2. Smithers, "Why Do So Many Americans Think They Have Cherokee Blood?"

in Cherokee villages and participated fully in Cherokee life. They learned the customs and habits of the Cherokee. "All it took was a drop or two of Cherokee blood to be considered Cherokee," wrote one descendant. "Some say that Cherokee is not a matter of blood at all, but *a thing of the spirit*."[1]

Communal Living

The Cherokee were a largely agricultural people in their early history. Their primary crops were corn, beans, and squash. The fields used to grow these crops were not owned by individuals or families. Rather, the women of a village would work together on communal farms. Women and children also foraged in nearby forests for wild berries, nuts, and fruits to supplement their diet. The plants provided both food and medicines to treat a wide variety of illnesses.

Men and women had different roles and responsibilities. While the women tended the fields and took care of their children, the men were hunters. They often left for months at a time on the hunt for deer, wild turkey, bear, and other animals. The meat from these animals was an important part of the Cherokee diet. The skins were used for clothing and tools. As the areas near Cherokee lands were settled by English colonists, the Cherokee also traded the skins for European tools and later for guns and ammunition. Additionally, the Cherokee men fished in rivers and streams with spears and nets.

An equally important role for men was warfare. War was routine, particularly among groups competing for the same hunting grounds. Encounters in the hunting grounds often resulted in injuries or deaths. The Cherokee believed that it was important to maintain balance in the world: If a member of the tribe was killed, the only way to restore balance was to avenge their death by taking the life of someone in the killer's group. This responsibility fell to the clan. For instance, if a Creek warrior killed a member of the Bear clan, the Bear clan would have to avenge the death by killing a Creek. Of course, this would create an imbalance in the minds of the Creeks, who more likely than not would avenge this death with yet another. To early Europeans, this appeared to be a destructive cycle of violence.

THEY MADE HISTORY: SEQUOYAH

Sequoyah (sometimes spelled Sequoia, or Sikwayi in Cherokee) was a Cherokee leader who made an important contribution to his people's culture by inventing their system of writing. He worked on his Cherokee syllabary from 1809 to 1821; before that time, the Cherokee kept records through memory only, passing down stories, advice, and historical events through the generations by word of mouth. Sequoyah believed it would be easier for the Cherokee to advance in the white man's world if they had a written language like white people did. The syllabary worked like an alphabet, but each of the 85 characters represented a different speech sound in the Cherokee language. This made it relatively easy for Cherokee to learn to read and write in their own language. In fact, it was so easy to learn that it spread quickly throughout the Cherokee Nation.

Soon after the introduction of Sequoyah's system, the Cherokee Nation began publication of the *Cherokee Phoenix*, which printed articles in both English and Cherokee. From its inception in 1828 until it was forced to close in 1834 due to lack of funds, the *Cherokee Phoenix* (later called the *Cherokee Phoenix and Indian Advocate*) provided a critical means for the Cherokee people to share news and voice opinions. The newspaper was also used to print new laws and meeting notices as well as to bring together the far-flung Cherokee as one nation, united in their defense of their homeland, values, and customs. Sequoyah's syllabary also made it possible for the Cherokee to adopt a written constitution, which was based on the Constitution of the United States. According to the National Park Service,

Cherokee Government

The early Cherokee government was centered within clans and villages. For example, clans would make sure that a person was properly punished for wrongdoings. To address issues that affected the entire village, each village had a council made up of one elder

Shown here is Sequoyah with the Cherokee syllabary.

the Cherokee language is "considered one of the cultural masterpieces of modern times."[1] To honor Sequoyah, a type of redwood tree—the giant sequoia—was named after him in the mid-1800s.

1. "The Giant Sequoias of California: Discovery and Naming of the Sequoias," National Park Service, modified February 2, 2007, www.nps.gov/parkhistory/online_books/cook/sec3.htm.

from each clan. Only men served on the councils, but older women often earned significant respect from younger villagers. Decisions were made by consensus, or the general agreement of the group. All members of the council were welcome to give opinions and argue their point of view. "This does not mean that the Cherokees considered all opinions to be equal," historians have noted. "Leadership

HISTORY HAPPENED HERE: THE SOUTHEAST

The Cherokee were one of the largest groups of native peoples living in the Southeast, but there were many other groups too. The Cherokee, Choctaw, Chickasaw, Creek, and Seminole became known among European settlers as the "Five Civilized Tribes." For the most part, these groups got along well with the Europeans and even began to adopt parts of European culture.

The Choctaw lived in present-day Mississippi. They were great farmers who grew so much of their pumpkin, corn, and bean crops that they were able to trade and sell them. The Creek, or Muscogee, made their home in modern Georgia and Alabama. They were commonly known as either Upper Creek or Lower Creek depending on where they lived. The Chickasaw lived in what are now the states of Mississippi and Alabama and may have once been joined with the Choctaw. The Chickasaw were known to be great warriors and often raided other groups to their north. The Seminole lived in present-day southern Georgia and Florida, including parts of the Everglades. They were partly made up of Creeks who had fled south. The influence of these groups can still be seen in various aspects of life in these Southeastern states, such as cultural demonstrations, museum exhibits, place names, and monuments.

All five tribes were subject to forced removal from their homelands at the hands of the US government. Their journeys were all difficult, despite the fact that the Cherokee's journey west is most closely associated with the Trail of Tears.

in a Cherokee community, in fact, rested with a person who could inspire followers rather than someone born to office."[2]

In addition to the village government, representatives from different villages met to decide issues of importance to all Cherokee. By the early 1800s, the Cherokee Nation had an established system of representative government. Numbering between 16,000 and 17,000 people, the Cherokee Nation was the most populous in the Southeast. They also had a force of roughly 6,000 warriors, making them one of the most powerful nations as well.

Trade and Disease

Warfare and politics were not the only reasons the Cherokee left their villages; the hunt for food often took Cherokee men many miles from their homes. Cherokee also traveled along waterways and footpaths to trade with other Native American groups living in the southeastern United States. Soon after the arrival of Europeans, the Cherokee Nation began to trade with them as well. Early on, the Cherokee traded beaded goods for woolen blankets and coats. Later traders exchanged deerskins for a variety of European goods, including metal farm implements and other tools as well as guns and ammunition. These were more effective for hunting and warfare than the stone knives and axes the Cherokee had been making themselves for many years.

Trade with the Europeans forever changed the nature of life for the Native Americans. Many tribes soon became dependent on trade with the white settlers, requiring metal axes, hoes, knives, and firearms. These upgraded tools made their lives much easier, but it also forced many Native American tribes into frequent contact with European settlers.

European traders brought more than items to be traded. They also brought deadly diseases. Smallpox, measles, and other diseases spread rapidly through Native American villages. Like all Native Americans, the Cherokee people had never been exposed to these European diseases and their bodies had no way to fight them. In addition, the Native American medicine men did not know how to treat the new diseases. Within just a few decades, diseases killed thousands of Cherokee. In some areas, entire communities were wiped out within just a few years of the first contact with Europeans. In 1738, a smallpox epidemic spread rapidly through Cherokee villages. Some historians estimate that the Cherokee Nation lost as much as half of its population within a year.

Forming Alliances

As soon as they were set up, the colonial governments sought alliances with Native American groups for both trade and warfare

Smallpox was one of the biggest killers of Native Americans, and it caused its victims great suffering before they died. Shown here are two girls from the Ho-Chunk tribe suffering from smallpox.

purposes. The colonists often took advantage of age-old rivalries between tribes to drive Native Americans off their homelands. In 1711, for instance, the Cherokee Nation and several other tribes joined the colonists in a war against the Tuscarora tribe in present-day North Carolina and South Carolina. The Tuscaroras had already been devastated by conflict and disease. Only about 5,000 of the 25,000 Tuscaroras who had been living in America prior to European contact remained. In what became known as the Tuscarora War, which raged for four years, thousands of Tuscaroras were killed or captured. Many of the prisoners—most of them women and children—were sold into slavery. In the peace treaty, the Tuscarora tribe ceded, or gave up, much of its land in North Carolina and South Carolina to the colonists. The majority of the remaining Tuscaroras moved north to take refuge among the Iroquois tribe—distant relatives in New York and Canada. Through such wars and skirmishes, Native American groups throughout the colonies were removed from their lands.

In exchange for their alliance with the colonies, the Cherokee received a promise of peace as well as a large payment of guns and ammunition. In 1721, the Cherokee Nation signed another treaty with South Carolina, establishing a fixed boundary between Cherokee land and the colony. This was the first land cession made by the Cherokee to the Europeans.

Native Americans also got involved in ongoing conflicts between European groups in the New World. In general, the French fur traders and colonists tended to treat Native Americans better than the English did, so Native American tribes tended to side with the French when conflicts broke out. The British colonists feared an alliance between France and strong Native American groups, such as the Cherokee. In 1730, Sir Alexander Cuming, a Scottish nobleman, visited Cherokee towns and met with their chiefs to win their friendship. He convinced several prominent chiefs and their councils to declare their allegiance to the king of England. When he returned to England, seven Cherokee representatives accompanied him to meet with King George II.

Sir Alexander Cuming (*center*) visited the Cherokee to gain their trust and friendship.

During their visit to England, the Cherokee signed a treaty again pledging their allegiance to and alliance with Britain. The treaty declared that any enemies of the English were also the enemies of the Cherokee. It further decreed that the Cherokee would treat the English as their own brothers and be prepared to fight against anyone who opposed them. This was a major turning point in Native American affairs with Europeans.

A Period of Conflict

When war broke out between France and England in 1754, the Cherokee Nation formally allied with the British, but many warriors fought alongside the French. In the colonies, this conflict became known as the French and Indian War.

The French and Indian War had a devastating effect on the Native Americans who lived in its path. Most Native American nations fought alongside their European allies, often engaging in more dangerous missions than their European counterparts. Thousands died fighting on one side or the other. Entire villages moved westward to get away from the conflict.

The Cherokee were among the many native groups that lost land because of the war. On February 10, 1763, the French and the British signed the Treaty of Paris, ending the nine-year-long war. England had decisively defeated France, and in the treaty, France ceded all the land in North America that was claimed by both France and England. During the war, the Cherokee Nation had shifted its official alliance from Britain to France, so it was considered a defeated power in the peace treaty. Britain claimed Cherokee land as part of the treaty it signed with France.

For many native populations, the loss of the French-claimed land east of the Mississippi was the worst outcome of the war. It meant the loss of France as a European power to balance England's power in North America. Without an additional power on the continent, there was nothing to stop the British from expanding unchecked into Native American territory.

During the French and Indian War, various Native American groups fought each other as well as the French and British. Shown here is a 1903 painting that depicts French-allied Native Americans being led in an ambush against the British.

Forced to Cooperate

In the years that followed the French and Indian War, the Cherokee and other Native Americans in the southeastern United States signed a series of treaties. The treaties were signed by the tribes in good faith, but with heavy hearts. "Every treaty was essentially forced upon the Cherokee," one historian wrote, "and only signed because they were assured that no further cessions would be demanded."[3]

Native American leaders believed that signing a treaty—even if it meant giving away some of their land—was the only way to form a permanent border that would protect the remaining land from the encroachment of white settlers. The treaties were largely useless, however. Even where colonial governments tried to enforce the treaties, settlers simply ignored them and built homes and farms on the land that had been identified as belonging to the Cherokee Nation. White settlers raised local militias to protect themselves against raids by Cherokee who were trying to protect their own land. Recognizing that they were outnumbered and outgunned, the Cherokee leaders signed more treaties, giving up the now-occupied land in exchange for the settlers' promise to honor the new boundary.

However, the Cherokee themselves sometimes ignored the treaties. In the Transylvania Purchase of 1775, for example, the Native Americans ceded lands north of the Cumberland River, including most of what is now Kentucky. A loosely affiliated group of Cherokee called the Chickamauga refused to honor the treaty. Over the next several decades, the Chickamauga continually raided English settlements. This further angered white settlers, who did not know or care about the differences between Native American tribes. An increasing number of settlers believed that the only way to protect themselves from such attacks was to remove Native Americans from the land completely.

Another War

The Cherokee blamed the settlers—not the British government—for the ongoing loss of their land. For this reason, when war broke out between the American colonists and Great Britain in 1775, many Cherokee sided with Great Britain. Colonists called loyalists, who were fighting for Britain, got help from Cherokee villages, and Cherokee warriors joined British troops. Patriots in the South struck back; for example, South Carolina offered a bounty for the scalps of Cherokee warriors. Throughout the South, troops raided Cherokee villages, burning their houses and fields. By the end of the summer of 1776, the Americans had destroyed more than 50 towns and left the Cherokee people without food and shelter. Hoping for peace, the Cherokee signed a treaty giving up land in North Carolina. The land ceded included areas where Cherokee towns and villages existed—some of which had been home to the Cherokee people for centuries.

In 1783, representatives from England and the new United States signed the Treaty of Paris to end the American Revolution. In the treaty, England ceded all of the land that had been the 13 colonies to the United States. The territory of the Cherokee Nation, like that of other Native American groups, was included in this land. One of the first challenges for US leaders was to decide how to deal with this land and the native groups living on it. Among the issues to be decided was what level of government—state or federal—had the authority and responsibility to deal with the Native Americans.

Both North Carolina and Georgia granted Cherokee lands to their citizens in 1783. The Cherokee fiercely protested, claiming that the states had no right to give their land to anyone. Although most Cherokee worked to resolve the disagreement peacefully, the Chickamaugas took up arms against the white settlers who moved onto their land and the militia who fought back to protect these settlers.

The new federal government sought to put an end to the conflict between states and Native Americans. In 1785, commissioners from the US government met with Cherokee representatives at Hopewell, South Carolina. The resulting Treaty of Hopewell defined the boundaries of Cherokee territory and recognized the right of the Cherokee Nation to expel whites who tried to settle on Cherokee land. The treaty accomplished little, however. Both Georgia and North Carolina refused to recognize the treaty, saying that the

FROM THE SOURCE: "WASHINGTON TO SENATE ON CHEROKEE INDIANS"

The US Constitution grants the president of the United States the ability to make treaties with the approval of the Senate. It was President George Washington who decided that this power would be used to make agreements with Native American groups, just as it would be with any other nation. However, the expanding country and the young, somewhat weak federal government made these treaties hard to enforce. Many settlers simply ignored the boundaries.

In a letter to the Senate in 1790, Washington acknowledged problems with white settlers moving onto Cherokee land past the boundary created by the Treaty of Hopewell. However, he did not commit to honoring past or future agreements or even firmly state his intention to pay the Cherokee for their land:

The White people settled on the frontiers ... openly [violating] the said boundary by intruding on the Indian

federal government had no right to interfere in the states' relationships with the Native Americans within their borders. Tensions between the federal government and the southern states would continue for decades, with the Cherokee caught in the middle.

Trying to Work Together

The US Constitution, which was ratified in 1789, gave authority over "Indian affairs" to the federal government. The next year, Congress passed a law requiring all purchases of Native American land to be made by treaties between tribal leaders and commissioners appointed by the US government. Federal lawmakers hoped this would prevent more conflicts between states and the US government about Native American policies. They wanted to reduce the risk that states would make promises to Native American groups *lands ... The United States in Congress ... did issue their proclamation forbidding such unwarrantable intrusions and [telling] all those who had settled upon the hunting grounds of the Cherokees to depart with their families [immediately] ...*

I state the following questions and request the advice of the Senate thereon.

1st. Is it the judgment of the Senate that overtures shall be made to the Cherokees to arrange a new boundary so as to embrace the settlement made by the white people since the treaty of Hopewell in November 1785?

2. If so, shall compensation ... be made to the Cherokees for the land they shall relinquish, holding the occupiers of the land accountable to the United States for its value?

3dly. Shall the United States stipulate solemnly to guarantee the new boundary which may be arranged?[1]

1. George Washington to Senate, August 11, 1790, Library of Congress, www.loc.gov/teachers/classroommaterials/presentationsandactivities/presentations/timeline/newnatn/nativeam/gwletter.html.

that conflicted with federal policies.

Henry Knox, President George Washington's secretary of war, was responsible for Indian affairs. He did not agree with how policy for dealing with Native American groups was being shaped. Knox felt the federal government did not respond properly to the "disgraceful violation of the treaty of Hopewell, with the Cherokees [by] the lawless whites."[4] Knox favored putting soldiers within Cherokee territory to protect the Native Americans living there from white settlers who refused to recognize the legal land boundaries set by the treaty.

Knox, however, was in the minority. Most members of the new United States wanted as much land as they could get their hands on. Washington and other prominent politicians believed that the best solution was for the Cherokee to assimilate into white culture.

Henry Knox thought the new American government should treat the Native Americans fairly and prevent white people from settling in their lands. However, most other government officials disagreed with him.

Essentially, assimilation is a process in which one group—in this case, the Native Americans—takes on the customs and beliefs of another—in this case, white Americans. While this policy would ease some tensions between the groups, Native Americans would be losing part of their ancient cultural identity.

Part of Washington's strategy involved making peace with Native American tribes. In 1791, the US government signed a treaty that guaranteed the Cherokee Nation a huge tract of land. This land lay within the states of Georgia, North Carolina, South Carolina, and what would become Alabama, Kentucky, and Tennessee. One of the goals of the 1791 Treaty of Holston was that the Cherokee would become farmers instead of hunters—a way of life that white Americans viewed as more civilized because it was the way they themselves lived. In order to make this happen, the United States agreed to give the Cherokee people farm equipment, tools, and draft animals, as well as people to show them how to use the tools they'd been given. One historian described the appeal of the treaty to Native Americans: "The Cherokee gave up large parts of their hunting grounds in the treaty, but they were promised some advantages; in exchange for the land, the treaty promised them peace, the protection of the federal government, an annual payment, and tools useful for farming."[5]

The idea of assimilation was not new, and the Cherokee seemed more likely to assimilate than other native groups. From the earliest contact with Europeans, the Cherokee had adopted many of the ways of their white neighbors. White people married into the Cherokee Nation, and Cherokee occasionally moved off traditional lands into log cabins and brick houses. An increasing number of Cherokee wore European-style clothing and practiced Christianity. Assimilation increased after the American Revolution, as the federal government believed it would enable Native Americans and whites to live in harmony. However, the federal government failed to recognize how much the Cherokee valued their culture. They also did not realize how fiercely the Cherokee would fight to be allowed to keep it.

How You See History

1. How do you think life would have been different for Native Americans if Europeans had never arrived in what is now the United States?
2. Imagine if your culture had no written language. How do you think life would be different for you?
3. What do you think would have happened if the United States had not adopted a policy of assimilation?

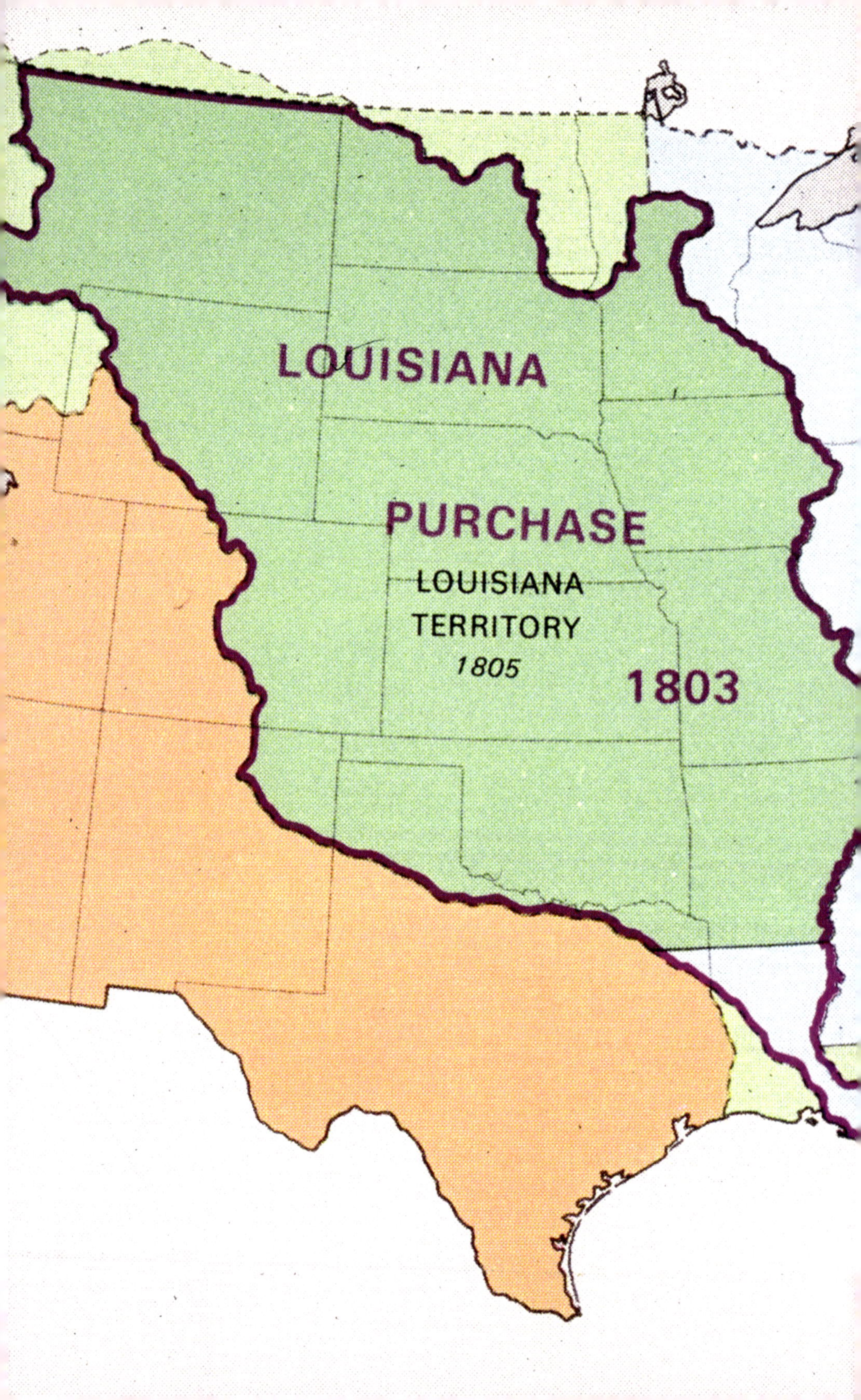

LOUISIANA
PURCHASE
LOUISIANA
TERRITORY
1805
1803

CHAPTER TWO

FIGHTING FOR A WAY OF LIFE

While the United States was trying to encourage Native Americans to assimilate into white culture, native people were trying just as hard to keep their culture and way of life as intact as possible. They did not want to give up their heritage to be part of the United States; they wanted to remain free and equal—sovereign, or independent, nations that worked with the United States government instead of being conquered by it. However, the United States continued to break its promises, making life harder for the Native Americans.

In 1790, Congress passed the Indian Trade and Intercourse Act, the first of six laws that became known collectively as the Non-intercourse Act. This law made it illegal for individual people or states to negotiate treaties with Native American groups. According to this law, only the federal government could make treaties with them, just as only the federal government was allowed to make treaties with other countries. From that point forward, all purchases of land from the Native Americans had to be arranged through treaties negotiated by tribal leaders and representatives appointed by the president. The Indian Trade and Intercourse Act of 1790 and the other acts that followed acknowledged that the

◀ The Louisiana Purchase took place in 1803 when Thomas Jefferson bought a large amount of land, including what is now the state of Louisiana, from the French. The government saw this land as a good place to get the Native Americans "out of the way"—at least, until American settlers started moving west.

US government viewed the Native American nations as sovereign entities, which meant they governed themselves.

The federal government felt this law was a necessity. From the start, the framers of the US Constitution had worried about negotiations with Native American groups. One major concern was that states would interfere. Because Native American nations did not fall neatly within one state, having different states negotiate their own independent treaties to set boundaries could result in conflict and confusion. In the Constitution, which went into effect in 1789, the framers gave sole authority over Native American affairs to Congress and the president. The 1790 trade act simply took that authority one step further.

The United States has negotiated, signed, and ratified almost 390 treaties with Native American groups. Despite the view that these groups were separate nations, many of these treaties were ultimately disregarded whenever the US government decided the new nation needed more land.

Disregarding the Federal Government

Not everyone agreed that the federal government should have sole authority over Native American affairs. Some southern states rebelled against the federal government's authority and continued to try to rid themselves of any Native Americans within their borders. According to the US Constitution, federal laws overrule state laws. In other words, states cannot pass laws that conflict with federal laws. When it came to Native American policy, however, several states—most notably Georgia—simply ignored federal laws.

The federal government sought a peaceful solution to the ongoing conflict between southern states and Native American groups. US leaders wanted to avoid war with powerful Native American groups and thought that negotiation was a better approach. This meant, however, that they would have to put a stop to white encroachment on the land that was promised to the Native Americans in treaties.

The colonial charters of North Carolina and Georgia did not outline a western border. To those living in these states, this meant that their lands extended west to the Mississippi River and perhaps beyond. Thomas Jefferson, who became president in 1801, thought that the answer to Native American conflict might lie in these vast tracts of open land far from white settlements. In 1802, he signed an agreement with the state of Georgia. In exchange for the federal government's promise to remove the Native Americans from within Georgia's borders, Georgia gave the federal government its claim to any land west of the Mississippi River. Jefferson's agreement did not include a set date for removal. Rather, the federal government said that it would obtain the land as soon as possible.

A New Way of Life

In part because of the federal government's assimilation policies, many Cherokee lived much like their white neighbors did by the early 1800s. They abandoned their deerskin dress for European-style clothes made of cotton. Some attended schools run by missionaries and embraced Christianity. With the loss of their hunting grounds, Cherokee men gave up hunting and began to work their farms, using plows and draft horses donated by the US government. In addition to the customary corn, beans, and squash for their own consumption, they planted cotton and wheat to be sold at market. Cherokee women gave control of the farms to their husbands and sons and took up spinning and weaving.

As the Cherokee people became used to white people living around them, the ways the Cherokee governed also changed. Their justice system gradually became more like that used by local governments within Georgia and South Carolina. For example, the Cherokee Nation had always relied on its clan-based system to settle issues between individuals. In the early 19th century, though, the Cherokee passed new laws to protect property. The first recorded Cherokee law was passed in 1808. This law established a police force to prevent the theft of horses and protect property rights.

In many ways, the Cherokee were similar to the white people living in the South. They lived peaceably among whites and prospered on their farms and in their businesses. Like their white neighbors, some Cherokee farmers used black slaves as labor on their farms; by the 1860s, more than 4,000 black slaves had Cherokee owners. The plantations of wealthy Cherokee looked much like those of white Southerners. Unlike white plantation owners, however, the Cherokee plantation owners, regardless of how wealthy they became, worked in the fields with their slaves.

In the villages, the Cherokee people ran stores, gristmills, and sawmills. The Cherokee Nation also had a museum, schools, and a library. The missionaries living among them boasted that the number of Cherokee who could read was higher than the number of white people around them who could read. Perhaps more than any other Native American nation, the Cherokee people assimilated into white American culture.

Still Facing Discrimination

Despite the Cherokee Nation's strides toward assimilation, many Americans remained distrustful of the tribe. They believed that Native Americans were an inferior race. One Georgian in Congress referred to the Cherokee people as uncivilized animals.

In addition, many white people were frightened of Native Americans. Their fears were enhanced by graphic—and often fake—stories of Native American raids on villages. They heard about the kidnapping of women and children and the scalping of men. Not surprisingly, they did not want any of these Native Americans to live where they planned to build their homes and raise their families.

Meanwhile, the population of the United States soared. White settlers continued to illegally encroach on Cherokee lands, clearing woods and building homesteads on land the Cherokee had been promised. Throughout the South, cotton plantations were springing up, bringing riches to those who had land and used slave labor. Future white plantation owners looked for fertile land, putting serious pressure on the Native Americans who lived there. Southerners grew increasingly impatient with the federal government's promises to resolve the problem through peaceful negotiation. They believed assimilation was impossible. US leaders hoped the Native Americans living east of the Mississippi River would agree to exchange their land for new land in the West that had been acquired through the Louisiana Purchase of 1803, far away from white settlers. Some groups did so and left peacefully to join distant relatives elsewhere, but many tribes put up a fight, tired of broken promises and not wanting to give up the land they had lived on for centuries. Andrew Jackson, a Tennessean who served as a general in the army, was among the many people who believed the best way to remove the Native Americans from the land was by force.

An Alliance With the Army

The US Army often formed alliances with one Native American group to fight against a rival tribe. For many generations, the Native American groups in the Southeast had fought over territory and hunting grounds, so they often saw the removal of neighboring tribes as advantageous. It is likely that the Cherokee Nation saw the United States as a powerful ally. So, when US troops fought to push out the nearby Creek tribe in 1813, Cherokee warriors joined Jackson's forces.

Over the next two decades, the Native American tribes in the southeastern United States signed a series of treaties. Most of these treaties offered an end to the fighting if the Native Americans agreed to give over their land to the US government. Treaties with the Cherokee Nation in 1817 and 1819, the Choctaw tribe in 1820, and the Creek tribe in 1826 all contained parts that encouraged the groups to move west. This offer was formally endorsed with the Indian Removal Act of 1830. This law set aside land west of the Mississippi River—in an unsettled area that was first known as Indian Territory and then, later, the state of Oklahoma—in exchange for Native American land in the Southeast. Through the treaties, the United States gained control of massive portions of Alabama and Florida, as well as parts of Georgia, Tennessee, Mississippi, Kentucky, and North Carolina.

Faced with constant hostility and pressure from whites, many Native Americans saw moving as their only option. They could leave freely and take what the government had to offer, or they would be forced out and left with nothing. In 1810, small groups of Cherokee moved to present-day Arkansas. In an 1816 treaty, another 4,000

The Choctaw (*shown here*) were one of the tribes that signed a treaty with the US government and agreed to move west instead of continuing to fight.

Cherokee gave up their land in Tennessee in exchange for land in northwestern Arkansas. In addition, the United States promised to pay the Cherokee Nation $60,000, in annual payments of $6,000 over 10 years. During the following years, other Cherokee joined their western brethren. By 1820, more than 6,000 Cherokee were living west of the Mississippi.

Most Cherokee had no interest in leaving their homeland, however. The leaders of the Cherokee people in the Southeast believed they had already lost too much of their land to whites and took measures to protect the land that remained. This was complicated by the fact that ownership of the land was not always clear. Prior to white settlements, the Cherokee did not use ownership deeds showing who owned what parcel, or piece, of land. In 1817, the Cherokee Nation passed a law giving its leaders—the Cherokee National Council—the sole authority to sell land. Individual Cherokee were prohibited from selling their houses and barns. In 1829, the Cherokee Council strengthened its power by making death the punishment for breaking this law.

A Strong Cherokee Government

Facing land loss and complications with treaties, the Cherokee Nation strengthened its national government. In July 1827, Cherokee delegates met in New Echota, Georgia, to draft a written constitution. Much of the Cherokee Constitution mirrored the founding documents of the United States and the state governments. For instance, the Cherokee government was divided into three parts, similar to the US government: the legislative, executive, and judicial branches. The constitution divided the Cherokee Nation into eight districts and gave all male members over 18 years of age the right to vote. In October 1828, Cherokee voters elected John Ross as their principal chief—a position similar to the US president.

A primary concern of those writing the constitution was to ensure the authority of the Cherokee Nation. The Cherokee Constitution was careful to outline the boundaries of Cherokee land. It declared that all land within these boundaries belonged to the

THEY MADE HISTORY: JOHN ROSS

When the Cherokee Nation reorganized its government in 1828, John Ross was elected as its first principal chief. Ross held this position until his death in 1866. He led the fight against the removal of the Cherokee, tirelessly writing letters and editorials, meeting with leaders of the US government to plead his case, and working with lawyers to bring court cases against those who tried to trample the rights of the Cherokee.

Ross was only one-eighth Cherokee by blood, but he lived as a Cherokee for his entire life. Like many Cherokee, he adopted the ways of whites. Ross served as a lieutenant in the Creek War, siding with Andrew Jackson's troops to force out the Creek Native Americans. He also served as a translator for US agents negotiating treaties with Native Americans and for the missionaries who settled in and around Cherokee land. By the time the Cherokee were forced from their land in 1838, Ross had become one of the richest men in northern Georgia.

Ross lost his fight to stay on Cherokee land in the East. His beloved wife, whose Cherokee name was Que-ti, was one of the people who died on the Trail of Tears.

John Ross was one of the people who worked the hardest to try to come to a peaceful, legal agreement with the United States on behalf of the Cherokee.

Cherokee Nation in common—not to individuals. The constitution also declared that the Cherokee people living within these boundaries were subject only to the laws of the Cherokee Nation.

Many Americans saw the Cherokee Constitution as proof that the Cherokee could become—and were becoming—assimilated in some ways. This was the first time that a Native American group had written a constitution to govern itself. However, many did not like what the constitution said. The governor of Georgia was especially angry about the Cherokee Nation's claim to be a sovereign nation, which meant that the Cherokee were not subject to the laws of Georgia or the United States. State officials believed they had the right to enforce Georgia's laws on the land the Cherokee people claimed was theirs.

The Problem With Gold

As more and more whites moved onto the land claimed by the Cherokee, tensions mounted. In 1829, gold was found on Cherokee land in the northwestern part of Georgia, near what is today Dahlonega. Rumors of gold spread quickly, and white settlers rushed onto Cherokee lands to make their claims. Mining operations soon sprang up, attracting more gold miners. Within a year, thousands of people were working the Georgia mines, which were producing huge amounts of gold every day. In the face of such riches, the gold miners cared little that they were trespassing on Cherokee land.

Georgia became increasingly aggressive in pushing the Cherokee off their land. Despite federal laws stating otherwise, Georgia officials argued that they had a right to establish and enforce laws governing Native Americans within their borders. In 1828, the state passed laws that took away Cherokee rights. According to state laws, the Cherokee had no right to sue whites or testify in court. This made it impossible for Cherokee to defend their claims on their land.

Recognizing that they would get no help from the states, John Ross and a group of Cherokee representatives traveled to Washington, DC, to ask for help from Congress. The delegation asked that the federal government honor its treaties with the Cherokee and enforce the boundaries between Georgia and the Cherokee Nation.

HISTORY HAPPENED HERE: DAHLONEGA, GEORGIA

Gold is still very much a part of Dahlonega's cultural identity; in fact, the town's motto is "It's Pure Gold." Visitors can kayak, fish, hunt, ride horses, go shopping downtown, and visit wineries and vineyards. However, the town's main attraction is the Gold Museum. It details the discovery of gold in present-day Dahlonega and the rush to Cherokee territory, although more focus is placed on the history of gold mining than the ways the Cherokee were affected. Dahlonega also offers visitors the opportunity to pan for gold in one of the town's creeks and hosts an annual Gold Rush Days festival the third full weekend in October.

Most members of Congress were indifferent to the plight of the Cherokee, but a few argued that the United States should keep its promises. In the Senate, Daniel Webster and Henry Clay argued before Congress that removal was unconstitutional and unwarranted. Davy Crockett, a US representative from Tennessee, also defended the Cherokee, despite the fact that the people in his home state were strong supporters of removal. Historians believe that Crockett's defense of the Native Americans cost him his political career.

Jackson Pushes for Removal

The struggle of the Cherokee and other Native Americans was made even more difficult when Andrew Jackson was elected president in 1828. Jackson, who did not see Native Americans as equal to whites, was a powerful believer in removal policies. In his first address to Congress, Jackson said, "I suggest for your consideration the propriety of setting apart an ample district west of the Mississippi [where Native Americans can learn] the arts of civilization."[1]

Jackson also did not consider the Native American tribes to be independent nations. He thought it was absurd for the US government to enter into negotiations with Native Americans: If tribes within the US boundaries refused to sell their land, the government should simply take it. In exchange, the government should offer them land west of the Mississippi, free from white interference. He argued that this would benefit not only the whites who wanted to settle on Native American lands but also the Native Americans themselves. Within a year of taking office, Jackson pushed the Indian Removal Act through Congress. The act gave the president

Andrew Jackson believed Native Americans were less civilized than white Americans. In reality, Native Americans had built complex civilizations hundreds of years before Europeans arrived in North America.

FROM THE SOURCE: ANDREW JACKSON'S ANNUAL ADDRESS

In the following excerpt from his 1830 annual address, Jackson explained how he believed the Native Americans would benefit from the Indian Removal Act:

> *The consequences of a speedy removal will be important to the United States, to individual States, and to the Indians themselves … It will separate the Indians from immediate contact with settlements of whites; free them from the power of the States; enable them to pursue happiness in their own way and under their own rude institutions; will [slow] the progress of decay, which is lessening their numbers, and perhaps cause them gradually, under the protection of the Government and through the influence of good counsels, to cast off their savage habits and become an interesting, civilized, and Christian community … Rightly considered, the policy of the General Government toward the red man is not only liberal, but generous.*[1]

1. Quoted in "Transcript of President Andrew Jackson's Message to Congress 'On Indian Removal' (1830)," OurDocuments, accessed November 21, 2019, www.ourdocuments.gov/doc.php?flash=true&doc=25&page=transcript.

the power to negotiate removal treaties by which tribes would give up their lands east of the Mississippi in exchange for lands to the west. Jackson believed that it was necessary to separate the Native Americans from the whites who were settling along the East Coast. "No state could achieve proper culture, civilization, and progress, as long as Indians remained within its boundaries,"[2] he wrote when he signed the act. Any Native Americans who did choose to remain would become citizens of their home states, subject to state laws alone.

In his 1830 address to Congress, Jackson called the Indian Removal Act a "benevolent policy." He added, "We now propose to acquire the countries occupied by the red men of the South and West by a fair exchange, and, at the expense of the United States, to send them to a land where their existence may be prolonged."[3]

Over the next several years, the federal government began carrying out Jackson's removal plan. During Jackson's administration, the national government negotiated 70 treaties with Native American groups. In many cases, the treaties were negotiated with a faction, or section, of a tribe, not with the chiefs elected by the entire nation. Most of the treaties included provisions in which Native American groups ceded land in the eastern United States in exchange for other land west of the Mississippi. By 1837—the end of Jackson's second term in office—more than 45,000 Native Americans had been removed from the East through this process.

Pleading Their Case

The Cherokee Nation continued to look for help from the US government. With Congress no longer seen as an ally, the Cherokee took their complaint to the Supreme Court. In *Cherokee Nation v. Georgia*, which reached the Supreme Court in 1831, the Cherokee Nation tried to stop the state of Georgia from enforcing state laws on Cherokee land. Supreme Court justice John Marshall wrote that Georgia's laws were "alleged [to] go directly to annihilate the Cherokees as a political society, and to seize, for the use of Georgia, the lands of the nation which have been assured to them by the United States in solemn treaties repeatedly made and still in force."[4]

Much to the dismay of the Cherokee Nation, the Supreme Court rejected their attempt to stop Georgia. The Court argued that, because the Cherokee people lived within US territory, they were a dependent nation. The US Constitution allowed only sovereign and independent nations to sue state governments. Although the US government had treated the Cherokee Nation as a sovereign nation, the Supreme Court did not believe that Native American nations had the same rights as other sovereign nations such as France or England. The Supreme Court denied the Cherokee the right to sue the government.

Just one year later, another case involving Cherokee authority was brought before the Supreme Court. Georgia state law required missionaries to obtain a license to live with and minister to Cherokee. Several missionaries believed that the state of Georgia would deny them a license because they supported the Cherokee in their fight against removal. Georgia learned that missionaries were living among the Cherokee with no license and ordered them to leave the state. The missionaries refused to do so. Eleven missionaries were arrested, convicted, and sentenced to four years of hard labor.

In 1832, the Supreme Court heard the case of *Worcester v. State of Georgia*. (Samuel Worcester was one of the missionaries.) The lawyer defending the missionaries argued that the state of Georgia had no authority over what happened on Cherokee land. The lawsuit contended that the land on which the Cherokee lived was not part of Georgia, so Georgia could no more make laws governing what people did within the Cherokee Nation than they could governing what people did in North or South Carolina. The law requiring missionaries to have a license was unconstitutional.

This time, the Supreme Court ruled in favor of the Cherokee. In the decision, Justice Marshall said that the US Constitution gave authority to regulate Native American affairs to the national government, not state governments. The Court agreed that Georgia was not allowed to impose laws within Cherokee territory.

In the end, though, the Supreme Court's ruling made no difference. President Jackson strongly disagreed with the decision, so his administration did nothing to enforce it. The federal government under Jackson did not stop Georgia or its citizens from taking Cherokee land and continuing to harass the Cherokee people when they protested.

Georgia had grown impatient with the federal government's promise to obtain Cherokee land within the state. In 1832, Georgia held two land lotteries that divided the Cherokee land into 160-acre (65-hectare) lots. In this lottery system, which had been used in other parts of the state, Georgia residents could enter their name to win the right to buy a lot for $4. The winners of the lottery were supposed to wait for the Cherokee to leave before taking own-

Supreme Court justice John Marshall supported the Cherokee Nation and their struggle to get the US government to enforce its promises. However, many of the other justices did not agree with him.

ership, but many moved onto the land right away. Some winners of the lottery sold their right to the land to others. Many of the buyers believed the deed they had won gave them legal ownership of the land, regardless of the Cherokee's claims. The Cherokee disagreed. They became increasingly angry about the influx of settlers, whom they viewed as invaders, on their land.

President Jackson continued to support the right of the state to claim the land. He believed the best solution was for the Cherokee to leave the land voluntarily, and he thought that harassing Cherokee residents might be the best way to persuade them to do so. "Build a fire under them," Jackson advised. "When it gets hot enough, they'll go."[5]

When white settlers and speculators realized that no one was going to stop them from seizing land, many more moved to Cherokee land and increased their harassment to get the Cherokee to leave. White settlers cut wood on Cherokee property, harvested their crops, and mined the gold found on Cherokee land. Some vandalized stores owned by Cherokee and stole horses or other property. Those who had purchased land in the lottery began to build homes and clear the land even though the Cherokee still claimed title to it. Some Georgians took over the homes where Cherokee families were already living.

Trying to Make Peace

The Cherokee Nation had always sought a peaceful solution. It had petitioned Congress and the Supreme Court. Although these attempts failed, John Ross and other Cherokee leaders continued to write letters to friends and Congress and go to Washington to plead their case. Elias Boudinot, the editor of the *Cherokee Phoenix*, wrote a series of editorials against removal, uniting the Cherokee and gaining new support. Many whites also spoke out in defense of the Cherokee. Women's groups and missionaries took up their cause, passing out petitions and writing letters of protest. Their efforts made little difference.

The Cherokee Nation continued to govern itself despite an 1830 law passed by Georgia that made it illegal for the Cherokee government to meet unless its purpose was to plan for removal. Anyone speaking out against removal was subject to arrest. The law also required whites living in the Cherokee Nation to declare allegiance to the state. A special police force was formed to enforce Georgia's laws within Cherokee territory. In response, the Cherokee Council decided that their government should be moved beyond Georgia's reach. The Cherokee leaders chose Red Clay, Tennessee, as the new government site in 1832. Red Clay was within the Cherokee Nation's boundaries and just across the border of

Georgia. It served as the site of the Cherokee government from 1832 until 1837.

Meanwhile, the Cherokee people continued to farm and run their businesses. They believed that the best way to prove they could live in peace was to continue to turn a blind eye to the wrongs they suffered at the hands of white people. They counted many white people among their tribe—those who had married into the Cherokee Nation numbered in the hundreds. There were also many white missionaries who lived among the Cherokee and counted them as friends. The Cherokee Nation pleaded with the white government and the white community for understanding and empathy.

Many Cherokee believed they would prevail in the end—that the United States would live up to the promises it had made and allow them to live on their land. As the 1830s wore on, however, an increasing number of Cherokee began to think they were fighting a lost cause.

How You See History

1. What policies do you think the federal government or state governments should have carried out to enforce the treaties they had made with the Native Americans?
2. Why do you think Andrew Jackson believed Native Americans would benefit from the removal policy even after they asked not to be relocated?
3. How do you think you might feel if someone told you that you had to move to a different state? What do you think you would do or say to make your feelings known?

CHAPTER THREE

A LOSING BATTLE

As time went on, the situation worsened for the Cherokee. They still faced white settlers on their land; this was true even for the people who had already voluntarily moved west. As conflicts increased, they looked to head even farther west. In 1828, they gave up their land in Arkansas for a piece of land in Indian Territory, farther away from white settlements. Western Cherokee have lived in this area ever since. By the 1830s, more than 4,000 Cherokee had already gone to live west of the Mississippi River.

Many of these early movers left their homes reluctantly. Some believed that they could find a better way of life, free of interference from the US or state governments. Others believed that the move was going to happen regardless of Cherokee wishes. Still others looked forward to an opportunity to start a fresh new life.

Disagreement Among the Cherokee

The Native Americans who stayed behind were under increasing pressure to move. By the early 1830s, this caused a rift in the Cherokee Nation in the eastern United States. A small but powerful faction had come to believe that the only way the nation could survive was to take the federal government's offer to exchange their land and move west. This faction became known as the Treaty Party.

John Ridge (*shown here*) and his father, Major Ridge, were two of the leaders of the Treaty Party.

The Treaty Party was led by some powerful Cherokee, including Major Ridge, his son John, Elias Boudinot—Ridge's nephew—and Andrew Ross, John Ross's brother. Many of these men were patriotic Cherokee who had fought hard to retain their native land. Major Ridge, for instance, was a full-blooded Cherokee—meaning all his ancestors were Cherokee—who had earned respect as both a warrior and a politician. He advocated for education and assimilation of the Cherokee and had sent his son to the finest schools available

FROM THE SOURCE: CHEROKEE NATION COUNCIL ADDRESS

The Cherokee Nation petitioned the United States to be exempt from the Indian Removal Act. This excerpt is from an 1830 address written from the council of the Cherokee Nation to the people of the United States:

> *We are aware, that some persons suppose it will be for our advantage to remove beyond the Mississippi. We think otherwise. Our people universally think otherwise ... We wish to remain on the land of our fathers. We have a perfect and original right to remain without interruption ... The treaties with us, and laws of the United States [guarantee] our residence, and our privileges and secure us against intruders. Our only request is, that these treaties may be fulfilled, and these laws executed.*
>
> *But if we are compelled to leave our country, we see nothing but ruin before us. The country west of the Arkansas territory is unknown to us ... it is not the land of our birth, nor of our affections. It contains neither the scenes of our childhood, nor the graves of our fathers.*[1]

1. "Two Documents on the Cherokee Removal," History Is a Weapon, accessed November 21, 2019, www.historyisaweapon.com/defcon1/cherokeeremoval.html.

to Cherokee people. Over the years, however, Ridge had come to believe that assimilation was an impossible dream.

John Ross was among those who argued against any treaty that would cede additional land to the United States. He was one-eighth Cherokee and seven-eighths white, but he and his followers thought of him as nothing but Cherokee. Ross's followers believed he would be able to convince white leaders to leave the Cherokee on their native land.

The anti-treaty group—those who continued to argue against removal—became known as the National Party. This group of Cherokee wanted to fight for their land. They believed that the government could not force the Cherokee people to leave against their will.

Conflict grew between the Treaty Party and the National Party. The two groups began pushing their individual beliefs as if they were the will of the entire Cherokee people. Each sent a delegation to Washington. Each held meetings with treaty commissioners from the federal government. In the fall of 1834, the two parties held separate councils. The Treaty Party drew up a resolution explaining its position on removal. Delegates expressed "the sorrowful conviction that it is impossible for them … to live in peace and comfort in their native region. [Our options are relocating] or sinking into a condition but little, if at all, better than slavery."[1]

The federal government used the Cherokee infighting to its advantage. In 1835, John F. Schermerhorn, a US treaty commissioner, invited the Cherokee to New Echota to craft a treaty. An estimated 350 of the roughly 17,000 members of the Cherokee Nation attended the meeting. In December 1835, officials of the US government and a small number of Cherokee settled on the terms of a removal treaty. The Cherokee did so reluctantly and sadly. "I have just signed my death warrant,"[2] Major Ridge announced after signing the treaty.

The Treaty of New Echota became the legal basis for the forcible removal of the Cherokee people. According to the provisions of the treaty, the Cherokee Nation ceded all its lands east of the Mississippi River in exchange for equal acreage—7 million acres (2.8 million ha)—in Indian Territory. The United States also agreed to help the Cherokee move and to support them for one year after their arrival

THEY MADE HISTORY: MAJOR RIDGE

Ridge was a Cherokee who was born in 1771 in the southeast of present-day Tennessee. Around 1800, he moved to Georgia, married a Cherokee woman, and set up a homestead. He fought in the War of 1812 alongside the Americans and was awarded the rank of major by Andrew Jackson, who was a general at the time. After that, Ridge started to use Major as his first name (Ridge was a translation of his Cherokee name).

Despite this loyal service, Ridge and other Cherokee were still targeted after Jackson became president. In 1832, when Georgia held a land lottery, Ridge's land was given to a white woman, who later sold it to a white man. Injustices such as these convinced Ridge that it was in the Cherokee's best interests to sign the Treaty of New Echota. He wrote,

> *We are few, and they are many ... We can never forget these homes, I know, but an unbending, iron necessity tells us we must leave them. I would willingly die to preserve them, but any forcible effort to keep them will cost us our lands, our lives and the lives of our children.*[1]

However, it was John Ross—not Major Ridge—who had received legal authority from the Cherokee Nation, so most Cherokee viewed the treaty as illegal and Ridge as a traitor. Ridge ended up being blamed for the Trail of Tears, and the year the surviving Cherokee arrived in Oklahoma after their journey on the Trail of Tears, his prophetic words

in their new home. The treaty further promised that each group of emigrants would be accompanied by wagons to carry their goods and a doctor with enough medicine for anyone who got sick along the way. The removal would take place within two years of the Senate ratifying the treaty. Families who did not wish to move could become citizens of their new state—with the notable exception of Georgia, which denied citizenship to anyone with Cherokee blood.

After he signed the Treaty of New Echota, Major Ridge was considered a traitor by most Cherokee.

about signing his death warrant came true: He, his son John, and his nephew Elias Boudinot were all murdered on June 22, 1839.

1. Quoted in John Ehle, *Trail of Tears: The Rise and Fall of the Cherokee Nation* (New York, NY: Anchor Books, 1999), p. 294.

Anger Over the Treaty of New Echota

Unfortunately for the Cherokee, they had no real way to decide the issue as a group. The state of Georgia would not allow the Cherokee to assemble or hold elections. The *Cherokee Phoenix* ceased publication in 1834, and there were no other newspapers Native Americans could use to debate or spread information. As a result, many Cherokee knew little about the pros and cons of agreeing to leave their land or what their real choices were.

Both the supporters of the treaty and those who were opposed to it claimed that they were the leaders of the Cherokee Nation and represented the wishes of the people. The federal government claimed that the representatives at New Echota were legally authorized to sign a contract with the US government. However, Principal Chief John Ross and members of the National Party disagreed. None of the treaty signers was a chief or a member of the National Council. Moreover, in Ross's opinion, the Treaty Party had gone against the will of the people. Ross and his followers protested the authority of the delegates to enter into a treaty, the terms of the agreement, and the manner in which it had been decided. This led to even more fighting among the Cherokee.

In early 1836, protest meetings against the treaty were held throughout the Cherokee Nation. The next Red Clay council meeting was attended by hundreds of Cherokee and lasted for three days. As a result of this massive protest, a delegation was sent to Washington to formally protest the Treaty of New Echota. The treaty would not become law until the US Senate ratified it, and Ross acted quickly to plead his case before Congress. In an impassioned letter, he denounced the signers of the treaty, saying that the Cherokee Nation did not recognize their authority and that they had acted against the wishes of the majority of their people.

The debate in Congress was heated. Some legislators argued that the treaty was not drafted in good faith and that it went against previous promises of the government. However, many legislators just wanted an end to the "Indian problem." They wanted to carry out the terms of the Indian Removal Act. On May 23, 1836, the Senate voted on the Treaty of New Echota; it was ratified by only one vote.

For the next two years, Ross pleaded with the government to reverse its decision. He went to Washington to seek advice on how to overturn the treaty. He believed the government officials would eventually see that the treaty was illegal.

During this time, Ross also called for a General Council of the Cherokee to discuss the Treaty of New Echota. In September 1836, thousands of Cherokee met at the Red Clay Council Grounds in Tennessee. Over the next several days, the council discussed the

HISTORY HAPPENED HERE: NEW ECHOTA

New Echota, Georgia, has much historical meaning to the Cherokee. It was where their constitution was drafted as well as where the treaty agreeing to their removal was signed. Today, the site is a national park. Visitors can enter 12 original and reconstructed buildings to learn more about the Cherokee and the Trail of Tears. These include the Council House, Court House, and the home of missionary Samuel Worcester. The visitor center includes an educational film, and nature trails allow tourists to walk around the area and get a feel for where the Cherokee lived.

Shown here is a reconstruction of the Council House in New Echota.

situation facing the Cherokee Nation. Ross told the attendees that the treaty was illegal. He described the land the US government had set aside for the Cherokee as dry and uninhabitable—and already occupied by other people. He sincerely believed the government would soon recognize the treaty as illegal and pleaded with the Cherokee to refuse to move off Cherokee land. At the end of the meeting, the Cherokee unanimously voted to reject the Treaty of New Echota.

Few gains were made over the following year. In the summer of 1837, the General Council met again. Again, thousands of Cherokee attended the meetings. With the deadline for removal getting closer, the emotions of the Cherokee were higher than ever. Once again, the council ended with a vote of support for resisting removal. At the meeting, an eight-member delegation was appointed to proceed to Washington to argue on behalf of the Cherokee Nation. To prove that the treaty did not represent the will of the people, Ross and his supporters gathered nearly 16,000 signatures on a petition of protest. Ross personally delivered the petition to Congress in the spring of 1838.

Ignoring Pleas for Justice

The Cherokee's final pleas were ignored. By this time, Martin Van Buren had been elected president, and he was prepared to follow through with the terms of Jackson's Indian Removal Act. It would be no easy task. An 1835 census conducted by the US government counted 16,542 Cherokee living east of the Mississippi River. Just over three-quarters of these—77 percent—were "full blooded;" the rest had at least one white ancestor. Whites who had married into the Nation and black slaves also lived with the Cherokee.

Worried that the Cherokee might stage an armed resistance, the federal government sent in troops to keep peace. General John E. Wool, who led the troops, was dismayed by the Cherokee's attitudes. It quickly became clear that the Cherokee were not going to leave voluntarily. Most Cherokee were following Ross's orders to resist removal in any way possible. "It is [pointless] to talk to a people almost universally opposed to the treaty and who maintain that they never made such a treaty,"[3] Wool wrote in an 1837 letter.

Wool pleaded with the Cherokee to leave voluntarily. He warned them that the US government planned to enforce the terms of the Treaty of New Echota regardless of their cooperation. If they did not leave voluntarily, they would be captured and forced to move west. The Cherokee who left before the deadline would benefit from the terms of the treaty—including new land, houses, and medical care—but those who refused risked losing everything. He called the people who were encouraging them to stay on the land, such as Ross and his supporters, "the worst of enemies [to the Cherokee]. Their advice, if followed, will lead to your certain destruction."[4]

General John E. Wool was not willing to force the Cherokee to leave their homes involuntarily, but he also did not ask the government to refrain from relocating the Cherokee.

In the end, Wool would not be part of this plan. He was willing to help those who enrolled for voluntary removal, but he did not want to violently force those who refused off their land. He saw everything the Cherokee people were giving up by leaving behind their homes, farms, businesses, and many other possessions. "They are being robbed and plundered … subjected to every species of oppression," Wool said. "Ninety-nine out of a hundred of them will go penniless to the West."[5] In 1838, he received approval for his request for a transfer, and General Winfield Scott took over command of the Cherokee removal.

Meanwhile, many white people feared that the Cherokee would resort to open war. The governor of Georgia claimed to have received a letter from a Cherokee who said that if the federal government would not leave them alone, the Cherokee would rise up and join the Creek and Seminole tribes in a bloody war against the United States. Historians believe that no such letter was ever sent; instead, Cherokee leaders and the councils meeting at Red Clay repeatedly committed to resolve the crisis without bloodshed.

The Treaty Is Enforced

Even though John Ross and his supporters attacked the actions of the Treaty Party, the signers of the Treaty of New Echota continued to defend their decisions. In 1837, Elias Boudinot published a pamphlet defending the actions of the Treaty Party. Because of his time editing the *Cherokee Phoenix*, Boudinot was well respected by the Cherokee. He explained that he signed the Treaty of New Echota because the nation was left with no other option. He pointed to the suffering of the Cherokee people and said that their situation was unfair. Boudinot was among the Cherokee who believed that removal was their only option. He also claimed that Ross was misleading the Cherokee by telling them they could fight the US government.

Over the next two years, hundreds of families left their homes and joined the groups of Native Americans who had moved west before them. Among the first to leave at this time were the signers of the Treaty of New Echota.

Most of the families who migrated in 1836 and 1837 were relatively prosperous. Their wealth helped protect them from the hardships of the long journey. They traveled by wagon train and took horses and livestock with them. Like those who would come after them, they traveled on narrow roads across the untamed countryside. They slept in their wagons. One of the greatest challenges—and the greatest risks—was crossing rivers, especially the Mississippi.

Captain B. B. Cannon, a member of the Tennessee Volunteer Infantry, led 365 Cherokee who chose to emigrate in the autumn of 1837. The government paid for this group to move west. Cannon's group followed trade roads through Tennessee, Kentucky, Illinois, Missouri, and Arkansas, traveling more than 800 miles (1,287 km) in all. The route was carefully planned to pass through towns where the group could frequently replenish supplies and make any needed repairs. It also passed near springs and waterways that would provide clean drinking water for people and animals.

In all, Cannon's journey took almost three months. Along the way, several other groups of Cherokee travelers joined up with the original group. Cannon reported having to stop for several days because of illness, but the fatality rate was far less than it would be for future Cherokee. Records indicate that 15 of the original 365 travelers died on the journey—a relatively low number compared to later groups.

As May 1838—the deadline for removal—approached, only a few thousand Cherokee had agreed to the terms of the treaty. The government estimated that more than 15,000 remained. Under the command of General Scott, the US Army was charged with forcibly removing the remaining Cherokee from their land. Though he was removing people from their homes, Scott's general orders were to treat the Cherokee gently and with as much respect as possible. Most soldiers followed Scott's orders and treated the Native Americans kindly. Scott later wrote that the roundup went well in most areas. In Georgia, however, the removal began badly. In that state, the Georgia Guard, an often-brutal force that cared little for the Cherokee or their needs, assisted the 2,000 troops under Scott's command. Scott later recalled:

> *The great difficulty was with the Georgians (more than half the army), between whom and the Cherokee there had been feuds and wars for many generations. The reciprocal hatred of the two races was probably never surpassed. Almost every Georgian, on leaving home … vowed never to return without having killed at least one Indian. This ferocious language was the more remarkable as the great body of these citizens—perhaps, seven in ten—were professors of religion.*[6]

Though Scott's soldiers tried to make the transition easy for the Cherokee, there are countless reports of Georgia Guard troops using cruel methods to force the Native Americans out of their homes. The soldiers caught many families off guard. Held at gunpoint, they had little time to pack their things or prepare for the journey. Some were forced from their homes with nothing but the clothes on their backs. Following the troops were whites who looted the possessions that the Cherokee were unable to take with them. The soldiers objected, but they had their hands full moving the Cherokee and could do little to stop the thieves.

A Time of Fear

Forcibly removing the Cherokee was difficult work. One soldier who participated in the removal later described the scene:

> *Men working in fields were arrested and driven to the stockades [wooden pens]. Women were dragged from their homes by soldiers whose language they could not understand. Children were often separated from their parents and driven into the stockades with the sky for a blanket and the earth for a pillow. The old and infirm were prodded with bayonets to hasten them to the stockades.*[7]

As the groups were rounded up, they were taken to forts, moving from one to another until they reached one of the three main depots: Fort Cass on the Hiwassee River, near present-day Calhoun, Tennessee; Ross's Landing in Chattanooga, Tennessee; and Fort Payne in Alabama. Rich and poor, elderly and newborns, frail, ill, pregnant, and wounded—all were forced into forts to await the journey west. The camps grew to accommodate the thousands of Cherokee awaiting departure. Many of the emigration depots were the size of a small town.

Some Cherokee voluntarily joined the groups, especially after it became clear that everyone was going to be forced to go no matter what. In a letter from 1838, one soldier wrote about what he saw as he accompanied hundreds of Cherokee from North Carolina to Tennessee: "We were eight days in making the journey (80 miles [129 km]), and it was pitiful to behold the women & children, who suffered exceedingly—as they were all [forced] to walk, with the exception of the sick."[8]

PAST MEETS PRESENT: THE TRUE MEANING OF SMEKDAY

In his fictional book, *The True Meaning of Smekday*, Adam Rex uses an alien invasion as a metaphor for the forced removal of the Native Americans. In the book, an alien race called the Boov invades Earth and forces all Americans to move first to Florida, then to Las Vegas, Nevada. When they protest that this is unfair because they were there before the Boov, the Boov say this will benefit everyone—just as Andrew Jackson suggested the Indian Removal Act would benefit the Native Americans as well as the white Americans. The book follows a young girl named Tip and the Boov she befriends as they fight to take back control of Earth.

The Cherokee had left behind everything they had ever known. Many were forced to leave with few possessions. No doubt they worried about neighbors, friends, and family who were in different camps. None of them knew what awaited them on the other side of their long and difficult journey.

How You See History

1. What would the Cherokee lose by assimilating?
2. Do you think the Cherokee would have been forced to move if the Treaty of New Echota had not been signed?
3. Why do you think the soldiers went along with forced removal instead of protesting it?

TOTAL NITROGEN
AVAIL. PHOS. ACID
AVAILABLE POTASH
50 LBS.
ROASTED
CALIFORNIA
PACKED 100 LBS. NET WEIGHT

CHAPTER FOUR

A DEADLY JOURNEY

Most Cherokee surrendered to their fate, but not everyone was aware of what was happening. Many of these Cherokee were "traditionalists" who lived in North Carolina, outside the boundaries of the larger Cherokee Nation. The traditionalists did not adopt the ways of the whites; instead, they continued to hunt and farm in the traditional ways of their ancestors. They lived as their ancestors had and knew little about the Indian Removal Act or the Treaty of New Echota. When they heard that their brethren were being rounded up, hundreds fled to the nearby mountains and woods.

Over time, the army lost interest in the few Cherokee scattered in these regions. The army gave up pursuit in 1842, and the remaining Cherokee were allowed to remain on the land unofficially. In 1848, Congress gave official recognition to the Eastern Band of Cherokee Indians. Today, there are more than 14,000 people belonging to the Eastern Band of Cherokee. They own land near the Great Smoky Mountains in an area called the Qualla Boundary, which they bought from the US government.

In addition to the Native Americans who hid from the army, another few hundred Cherokee remained behind because they were exempt from the army's order for removal. These Cherokee had been granted US citizenship and individual parcels of land through

◀ This photograph shows a woman grinding corn to make cornmeal at her home in the Qualla Boundary.

THEY MADE HISTORY: TSALI

Tsali lived outside the boundaries that the Cherokee Nation had established in its constitution. He was part of a group known as traditionalists, who lived simple lives farming and continuing the traditions of their ancestors. He cared little about the ways of whites and heard little news of the events leading up to the Trail of Tears.

Tsali was surprised when his brother-in-law warned him that soldiers were coming to take him and his family from their homes. He had no plans to alter his life because of this rumor. However, soldiers arrived at his family's small cabin and told them to begin heading toward an emigration depot. Tsali and his family gathered a few belongings and followed the soldiers toward the stockade. Along the path, a soldier prodded Tsali's wife with his bayonet. Tsali was infuriated. Speaking in Cherokee, he told his family that when he pretended to trip, they should grab the soldiers' guns and then run and hide. During the struggle, one of the guns accidentally went off, killing one of the soldiers. Tsali and his family fled into the hills.

The army was told to capture the Native Americans at any cost. Tsali, one of his sons, and his brother-in-law were captured and then executed by a firing squad. Rumors spread among the Cherokee that Tsali had turned himself in to the US Army in exchange for a promise that the army would leave the other Cherokee living in the mountains alone. This legend—the belief that Tsali had sacrificed his life so his people could remain in their homeland—helped fuel the resistance of the North Carolina Cherokee, even if it was not completely accurate.

treaties in 1817 and 1819. Because they were no longer members of the Cherokee Nation, they were not subject to removal.

History suggests that the Cherokee who remained behind were the lucky ones. For the most part, they were allowed to live much as they had in the past. Although they continued to face discrimination and hostility from their white neighbors, the Cherokee who stayed behind were spared the hardships of a 1,000-mile (1,609 km) westward march.

The plan seemed simple for the US Army to complete: Soldiers would lead groups of several hundred Cherokee, traveling first by steamboat down the Tennessee and Ohio Rivers to the Mississippi. Then, they would continue overland to Indian Territory. Groups would leave a few days apart so the army could refill supplies at stops along the way. However, the army did not count on Native American resistance or on the journey being longer and more difficult than expected.

Starting Out

On June 6, 1838, the first detachment of Cherokee and their few belongings were loaded onto long wooden flatboats of various sizes. Most of the boats had roofs over part of the hull, bunks inside for sleeping, and a small area for cooking. Despite these amenities, the flatboats were crowded and uncomfortable. Roughly 800 Cherokee in all were in this first group, including the black slaves they brought with them. Most of them were from Georgia. Two more groups soon followed, departing on June 13 and June 17. In all, these three groups included nearly 3,000 Cherokee. A US military officer, groups of assistants, and two doctors accompanied each group.

The flatboats were pulled by a series of steamboats on a winding river route along the Tennessee, Ohio, Mississippi, and Arkansas Rivers. These rivers, however, did not flow all the way to the Indian Territory. When they could no longer travel by boat, the Cherokee were herded into wagons and trains to continue the journey through Arkansas. There were not enough wagons for everyone, so the Cherokee who were healthy had to walk.

The trip took a heavy toll on the Native Americans. The summer of 1838 was swelteringly hot. Some of the boats got stuck on dangerous sandbars. The Cherokee often had to move from damaged boats onto boats that remained unscathed, resulting in unhealthy, overcrowded conditions. If one of these overloaded boats sank,

Shown here are birds sitting on a sandbar. Because sandbars are often hard to see, it was not uncommon for boats to run into them and be damaged or sunk during the Cherokee's journey.

hundreds of people could drown. Sickness and death were daily reminders of the perils of the trip.

Historians are not sure exactly how many Cherokee lost their lives, but they estimate that as many as 25 percent of the Cherokee on the earliest expeditions died of disease, hunger, and exposure. In some of the early groups, huge portions of the Native Americans who had set out from Tennessee never arrived at their final destination. After seeing so much death, some of the Cherokee escaped and made their way back east. Rumors of the small rations, rotten food, and harsh conditions frightened those who awaited passage.

On June 19, General Scott ordered the forced removals to be suspended until September 1. Scott planned to follow his orders to evacuate the Cherokee, but he was alarmed by the problems faced by the first groups. He had wanted the military operation to be fast, efficient, and compassionate, but it was impossible to meet all three of these goals. The weather wasn't cooperating, and the Cherokee were resisting by refusing to accept supplies or show up when they were ordered to. Scott hoped that waiting until autumn might address some of the problems the early groups had encountered. For example, fall rains would result in a higher water level in the rivers, making waterways easier to travel; there would be less risk of having boats get stuck on sandbars.

Anxious about the problems with the removal, the Cherokee Council sent a letter to General Scott requesting that the Cherokee people be allowed to plan and lead their own removal. General Scott agreed to the Cherokee's request to organize the remainder of the removal operation. The Cherokee elected John Ross and six others as the removal committee. Ross divided the Cherokee into different subgroups, ranging in size from about 700 to nearly 1,500. He also arranged for the groups to go overland so they could hunt along the way. Those who had money could also buy food and supplies to supplement the provisions that army contractors had placed along the route. In general, Ross believed it was better to be self-reliant than to depend on the army for provisions.

The committee negotiated a contract with the government that set a cost of $65.88 per person for the journey. This included the costs for wagons, horses, drivers, doctors, and other personnel. The contract also required the Cherokee to start their travels by September 1 and finish within two months, although an exception was made for those who were too ill to travel.

Harsh Conditions

The attitude of the Cherokee people improved under their own leadership, but they knew there would still be a long, hard journey ahead. The first of the 13 traveling groups organized by John Ross set out on August 28, 1838—ahead of schedule. The second began a few days later, on September 1, and the third just two days after that. Other groups followed over the next several months; the last group did not depart until December. Each detachment was led by a Cherokee leader and was accompanied by a doctor. The missionaries who had lived among the Cherokee also went with some of the groups. US soldiers rode alongside the procession and at the rear to make sure the group kept moving and did not turn back.

The official reports of the soldiers who accompanied the expeditions and letters sent to loved ones at home tell of the hardships the Cherokee endured on their journey. One soldier later recalled:

> *On the morning of November the 17th we encountered a terrific sleet and snow storm with freezing temperatures and from that day until we reached the end of the fateful journey on March the 26th, 1839, the sufferings of the Cherokees were awful. The trail of the exiles was a trail of death. They had to sleep in the wagons and on the ground without fire. And I have known as many as twenty-two of them to die in one night of pneumonia due to ill treatment, cold, and exposure.*[1]

There was not an "official" trail to the new Cherokee land. Each group found its own way. Most groups traveled north and west across Tennessee and Kentucky, across southern Illinois and Missouri, and then into northeastern Indian Territory. This trip required the Cherokee to navigate difficult terrain. They would walk over mountains and hills and through vast tracts of wilderness. They also had to cross several rivers, including the Mississippi.

Although the groups could decide their own route and each one had its own difficulties, the circumstances were generally the same. Later groups often caught up to the group before them, and sometimes the groups would mix. Some Cherokee would join another group when they found friends or relatives. Others might stay behind to rest for a few days and take up the march after a much-needed break from the difficult road. The men would sometimes leave their group to hunt for deer, turkey, or other food to supplement the army's inadequate rations. As a result, from the beginning, it was impossible to give an accurate count of how many people made the journey and how many died along the way.

Some of the wealthier Cherokee rode horses, and wagons carried those who were ill or too young to walk. Still, the vast majority of the Cherokee walked. Day after day, rain or shine, the Cherokee

had to leave some of their possessions behind to make room for them. When they came upon them too late, they would find rotting meat and wormy corn. Moldy hay made the horses and other animals sick. People became ill from drinking contaminated water. Some unethical contractors simply took the money the government paid them without actually using it to provide food. As winter set in, it became impossible to hunt to supplement the provisions the army provided.

Whereas the heat of summer had plagued the first expeditions, travel in fall and winter created its own problems. The trip was supposed to take about three months, but some of the groups took twice that long. Heavy rains slowed the groups and made travel difficult along the rutted country roads. Wagons became stuck in the mud. A white traveler from Maine who happened upon one of the Cherokee groups in Kentucky described the scene:

> *We found the road literally filled with the [travelers] about three miles in length. The sick and feeble were carried in wagons … a great many ride on horseback and multitudes go on foot. Even aged females, apparently nearly ready to drop into the grave, were traveling with heavy burdens attached to the back, on the sometimes frozen ground, and sometimes muddy streets, with no covering for the feet except what nature had given them.*[2]

As the travelers pushed westward, horses and other animals were lost. Wagon wheels broke. Sometimes wagons had to be abandoned completely, and people and possessions had to be either moved to those that remained or left on the path. The wagons became more and more crowded. As people got sick, older Cherokee and women with small children gave up their places in the wagons to those with greater need. However, riding in the wagons was not a comfortable experience; as they jostled over the deeply rutted roads, those who were ill suffered greatly.

The travelers were also at the mercy of the weather. There was no way to escape the rain, and the heat of the sun was not any better. For those who were sick, the harsh conditions made recovery almost impossible.

This 1951 painting by Native American artist Blackbear Bosin illustrates the harsh conditions people faced during the winter months on the Trail of Tears.

Most of the Cherokee had lived in the Southeast their entire lives. They were unprepared for the cold they encountered on the northern route. The army was supposed to provide blankets, but there were not enough to go around. To address this problem, the contingents often sent a small group of men ahead of the wagons to build fires at intervals along the road where the Cherokee could rest and warm themselves.

As winter set in, rivers froze, but often not completely. This made crossing them even more dangerous. Some detachments had to camp by a river's edge for days or weeks until the weather warmed up enough to make crossing the river possible. Several groups were stuck for a month in southern Illinois, waiting for the large chunks of ice in the Mississippi to melt.

Food became even more scarce during the cold winter. Thousands of people lacked warm blankets, warm clothes, or shoes. As people huddled together in makeshift shelters, illness spread rapidly. Many people died of diseases such as pneumonia and influenza. One expedition reported that 15 to 20 people died of exposure each night, due to their continuous time without shelter or other adequate protection from the poor weather.

Help and Harm

Some of the white people whom the Cherokee passed helped them along the way. Alerted by the missionaries who had lived among the Cherokee, some church groups collected food and blankets and brought them to where the Cherokee camped. Some white people opened their homes and churches to shelter the travelers. One family took in a Cherokee woman and her friends when she went into labor and provided a home for her and her baby boy for a few weeks after the birth.

However, not everyone was so friendly. Many whites were frightened of Native Americans and did not want them passing through their towns. It was not unusual for white people to take advantage of the Cherokee's situation. Stores charged unreasonably high prices for food and other supplies, and the Cherokee were sometimes forced to pay twice the toll of a white passenger for a ferry. A continuous stream of people waited to cross the rivers, and sometimes the ferry operators forced the Cherokee to wait until they had taken white passengers across. A broken wagon wheel might force the Cherokee to choose between paying an outrageous fee for a new wheel or leaving the wagon behind—along with the possessions they had in it. Some landowners demanded payment for crossing their land. Sometimes local residents made false claims of property damage and demanded that the Cherokee compensate them.

Alcohol caused additional problems. Merchants followed the bands of Cherokee, selling them whiskey and moonshine. The government agents accompanying the Cherokee often complained that the men were too drunk to continue their travels.

Escaping the Trail

Not all of the Cherokee obeyed orders to continue the westward journey. In fact, many people left without permission. This is part of the reason why no one knows exactly how many Cherokee died along the way. Some of the people who never arrived in Indian Territory with their groups had simply left the trail and escaped into the nearby wilderness. Seeing the long, dangerous road ahead, the escapees often tried to return the way they had come. Some took only what they could carry, but sometimes several dozen people would try to escape with wagons full of food and supplies.

The Cherokee leaders of the groups often did little to stop people who wanted to leave the trail. They left this task to the US troops. Some of the escapees were caught and continued the march under guard; others managed to escape into the woods.

One escapee was a North Carolina Cherokee named Junaluska (Tsunu'lahun'ski). He was among the 860 Cherokee who left under the leadership of a Cherokee Baptist minister named Jesse Bushyhead. Junaluska had served under the command of Andrew Jackson in the Creek War. He led a group of Cherokee who helped Jackson win the Battle of Horseshoe Bend in Alabama. He was also credited with saving Jackson's life during the conflict.

A few weeks into the journey, Junaluska and about 50 others informed Bushyhead that they intended to return to North Carolina. Bushyhead did not use force to stop them as they left the trail. Junaluska and 25 of his comrades were later captured near Knoxville, Tennessee, and taken as prisoners to Fort Cass. Junaluska was put in chains and sent back westward under guard of the soldiers who were to be stationed at Fort Gibson in the Indian Territory. He reportedly said, "If I had known that Jackson would drive us from our homes, I would have killed him that day at the Horseshoe."[3]

PAST MEETS PRESENT: THE MYTH OF THE "DRUNKEN INDIAN"

Since the first Europeans made contact with Native Americans, stereotypes about native people have developed and persisted. One of the most damaging and most pervasive is that Native Americans are more likely to develop an alcohol use disorder than people of a different race. This stereotype is highly damaging because it has been used for decades to imply that Native Americans are inferior to white people. As *Pacific Standard* magazine explained, "the [stereotype of the] drunken Indian male ... is often seen as morally deficient because of his inability to control himself, making him a menace to society."[1] One example is Injun Joe in *Tom Sawyer*—a Native American man who is always drunk and frequently violent.

However, recent studies have found that the idea that Native Americans are more likely to develop an alcohol use disorder is false. Firstly, white people drank frequently in Europe, and they brought alcohol with them to North America, where many of them drank to excess. Because Native Americans were already viewed as inferior, any drunken behavior they displayed was seen as worse than the behavior of white people—even if it was exactly the same. Secondly, only one study into the genetic role of alcohol addiction in Native Americans has been done, and it was later criticized for being flawed. No other research has found that Native Americans are genetically more likely to become addicted to alcohol. Although there are higher rates of alcohol use and alcohol deaths recorded in the native population, researchers believe this has much to do with the fact that many Native Americans live in poverty—a factor that is known to increase alcohol use regardless of race.

1. Roxanne Dunbar-Ortiz and Dina Gilio-Whitaker, "What's Behind the Myth of Native American Alcoholism?," *Pacific Standard*, modified June 14, 2017, psmag.com/news/whats-behind-the-myth-of-native-american-alcoholism.

In 1847, Junaluska was granted North Carolina citizenship and given a tract of land in the mountains. The many other Cherokee who escaped and settled in North Carolina were not as lucky, however. They had to wait many years to be recognized as citizens of the state.

Arriving in Indian Territory

On March 25, 1839, the last group of Cherokee arrived in the West. They had spent nearly half a year on the road. No one knows exactly how many deaths occurred during the journey. Elizur Butler, a doctor who accompanied one of the detachments, estimated that nearly one-fifth of the Cherokee population died. Other reports have the number closer to one-quarter. The trip was particularly hard on the elderly, children, and infants. The travelers died from colds, influenza, measles, fevers, dysentery, whooping cough, and cholera. Others died in accidents, from starvation, and due to other hardships of the journey. Many of those who died on the trail were hastily buried in unmarked graves; others had to be left unburied along the road. Not only had the Native Americans been forced to leave their homes, they had also lost many friends and family members along the way.

According to the African American Policy Forum (AAPF),

> *As with many racially motivated acts of oppression, the Trail of Tears has been treated differently by historians over time. Many historians agree that the Trail of Tears was at least a forced relocation. However, many historians and native peoples today prefer to use the term death march, especially in reference to the removal of the Cherokee in 1838. Others prefer the term genocide, or ethnic cleansing.*[4]

The terms genocide, death march, and ethnic cleansing all imply that the US government expected many Native Americans to die along the way—even before the journey began.

How You See History

1. Do you think it was ever possible for General Scott to achieve his goal of compassionately relocating the Cherokee? Explain your answer.
2. Could anything have been done by the government to minimize the suffering and death the Cherokee experienced on the trail? Explain your answer.
3. Why do you think there's disagreement about which term to use to describe the Trail of Tears? Which term do you think fits best?

INTRODUCTION
TENNESSEE
KENTUCKY

CHAPTER FIVE

THE AFTERMATH

The Trail of Tears was a deadly, traumatic ordeal for Native Americans. It is likely that they felt relieved when they finally reached Indian Territory. However, they still had difficulties to face. The Cherokee and other native groups removed to Indian Territory had no homes, businesses, or schools. Though the land looked similar to the land the Cherokee had lived on in the Southeast, they did not know the best places to plant crops, nor did they know the plant and animal life found in the region. The Cherokee Nation was united in one place again, but tension existed between those who had moved voluntarily and those who had been forced.

The Trail of Tears was just one part of the trials the Cherokee Nation faced in Indian Territory. Nonetheless, they have persevered for more than a century, dedicated to remembering all those who came before—including those who never made it to their new home.

Tension and Disunity

When the groups of Cherokee arrived in Indian Territory in 1839, they joined thousands of Cherokee who arrived before them. This was not necessarily a joyful reunion.

In 1819, the Cherokee in the East had formally disassociated themselves with those who would become known as the "Old

◀ This monument sits in Cherokee Removal Memorial Park in Tennessee. It is one of the few official Trail of Tears memorials in the United States.

Settlers" and refused to recognize them as part of the Cherokee Nation. Once they reached land in the West, the Old Settlers elected their own chiefs and passed their own laws. Naturally, this group of Cherokee wanted to continue following their own leaders and laws, even as more Cherokee joined them in Indian Territory.

The Old Settlers were greatly outnumbered when the thousands of eastern Cherokee arrived in 1839. In fact, the Old Settlers made up just one-third of the group. The new arrivals had no intention of subjecting themselves to the rule of the minority who were already established in Indian Territory. The eastern Cherokee wanted to continue to follow the written constitution, laws, and elected leaders of the eastern Cherokee Nation. Before leaving for their new western homes, they had even adopted a resolution declaring that the Cherokee Nation as they knew it would survive once they reached the West.

In April 1839, Principal Chief John Ross proposed that a joint council be held to create a new, unified government. On June 3, 1839, thousands of Cherokee met to discuss what should be done. John Brown, one of the chiefs of the Old Settlers, publicly welcomed the new arrivals—with one condition:

> *We joyfully welcome you to our country. The whole land is before you. You may go freely wherever you choose & select any places for settlement which may please you … Next July will be an election … for members of both houses of our legislature … At those elections you will be voters … [Meanwhile] it is expected that you will all be subject to our government & laws.*[1]

Although the eastern Cherokee were to be given the right to vote in the next elections, Ross was opposed to the suggestion that the eastern Cherokee would no longer be governed by the laws they had already written. This created a serious conflict between the Cherokee settlers.

Thus began a difficult negotiation process between the chiefs of the two factions. Ross rejected Brown's subsequent proposal that the two bands continue to be governed separately because he believed this would weaken their position with the US government, as well as create confusion and conflict among the Cherokee. As an alternative, he proposed having a committee of elected officials create the new laws for the unified Cherokee Nation. Three representatives would be elected by the western Cherokee, three by the eastern faction, and the remaining three would be selected by these six. The new laws would then be presented to the Cherokee people for approval. Brown worried that this would give the eastern Cherokee a clear advantage because they were in the majority.

One of the reasons it was important to decide who was in charge was because the US government owed the Cherokee money. The government had promised to pay the Cherokee for their land and to support them during their initial months in the Indian Territory. Each of the two factions believed that they should be in charge of the funds. The leaders of the Old Settlers wrote a letter to Montfort Stokes, the US agent in charge of the funds, requesting that he pay them instead of the new arrivals. The eastern Cherokee were outraged. The leaders of the eastern faction wrote their own letter to Stokes, asking that he not distribute any money until the Cherokee were officially united.

Revenge Against the Treaty Signers

The anger on the part of the easterners was fueled by the fact that the Old Settlers counted among their numbers the leaders who had signed the Treaty of New Echota. The eastern Cherokee believed that this treaty had robbed them of their land. They viewed the men who had negotiated the treaty as traitors and blamed them for the many hardships the Cherokee people had endured over the past several months. For this reason, several of the eastern Cherokee assassinated Major Ridge, John Ridge, and Elias Boudinot on June 22, 1839.

These swift killings had a number of consequences. Historian William G. McLoughlin wrote, "Their deaths caused an immediate panic among all members of the Treaty party, a [powerful] reaction by the federal government, and general horror among the white American public."[2] Word of the attacks spread quickly through the Cherokee community. Many supporters of the Treaty Party fled to Arkansas. Others took up arms and vowed revenge.

Friends and relatives of the victims blamed John Ross for the murders. They believed that Ross had ordered the killings. Stand Watie, the only assassination target who escaped being killed, had gathered a group to retaliate by killing Ross. Ross insisted that he did not know who the executioners were and expressed regret for the murders. Fearing for his life, he wrote to the American government to ask for protection. This was not needed, however, because hundreds of Ross's supporters converged at his home to defend him from any attempts on his life.

As a reaction to this gathering of pro-Ross Cherokee, however, former Treaty Party members assumed the armed men were planning more murders. It was their turn to appeal to the American government for help. Hoping to settle things without any more violence, federal troops were sent to Cherokee territory to help keep the peace.

On July 1, a meeting was held. Many former Treaty Party members, including Watie, were afraid to attend. Ross wanted to use this meeting to call a truce. He knew that the survival of the Cherokee Nation depended on peace between the warring factions. At the meeting, the council called for forgiveness for the murderers of the Ridges and Boudinot. The council then asked the signers of the Treaty of New Echota to come forward and apologize for signing the treaty. Eight men came forward, but the rest of the signers refused. Watie was among those who insisted that they had acted in the best interests of the Cherokee Nation.

Working Toward Unity

Despite the opposition he faced, Ross continued to work for Cherokee unity. A number of meetings were held to persuade Cherokee on both sides to vote for peace. Finally, on July 12, 1839, the Act of Union was adopted. The act stated, "We, the people composing the … Cherokee Nation, in national convention assembled, by virtue of our original and inalienable rights, do hereby solemnly and mutually agree to form ourselves into one body politic under the style and title of the Cherokee Nation."[3]

On September 6, the new council of the reunited Cherokee Nation held its first meeting in the new capital of Tahlequah, Oklahoma.

THEY MADE HISTORY: STAND WATIE

Stand Watie was born in 1806 in present-day Georgia. He believed that the Cherokee's best chance at survival was to cede their traditional homeland. Watie helped negotiate the Treaty of New Echota. He was among about 2,000 Cherokee who moved voluntarily to Indian Territory after the treaty was signed. After Watie was informed that the eastern Cherokee planned to kill the leaders of the Treaty Party for their role, he fled to Arkansas. He later returned to lead a faction of Cherokee who opposed John Ross and his leadership.

Later in life, Watie distinguished himself during the American Civil War. He organized and led a cavalry of Cherokee known as the Cherokee Mounted Rifles. These Cherokee fought diligently, not only against the Union forces but also against the Cherokee who had joined the Union army. He became one of only two Native Americans to achieve the rank of general in the Civil War. On June 23, 1865, Watie was one of the last Confederate generals to surrender to Union troops.

Stand Watie narrowly escaped assassination after the eastern Cherokee arrived in Indian Territory. He remained involved in Cherokee politics even after this scare.

FROM THE SOURCE: THE CHEROKEE CONSTITUTION

The Act of Union that was adopted in 1839 was the basis for the new Cherokee Constitution. This constitution remained in effect until 1975. It was rewritten partially to help the Cherokee gain more independence from the US government; until that point, the federal government had been appointing tribal chiefs and making rules for the Cherokee, even though they were supposed to be self-governing. The preamble of the 1975 constitution states:

> *We the people of the Cherokee Nation, in order to preserve and enrich our tribal culture, achieve and maintain a desirable measure of prosperity, insure tranquility and to secure ourselves and our posterity the blessings of freedom, acknowledging, with humility and gratitude, the goodness of the Sovereign Ruler of the Universe in permitting us to do so, and imploring his aid and guidance in its accomplishment—do ordain and establish this Constitution for the government of the Cherokee Nation.*[1]

1. Marilyn K. Nicely, ed., "Constitution of the Cherokee Nation of Oklahoma," University of Oklahoma Law Center, modified April 2, 1998, thorpe.ou.edu/constitution/cherokee/index.html.

The delegates signed their newly drafted constitution and elected John Ross as principal chief. However, not everyone accepted the sovereignty of the new government. For many years, the Old Settlers refused to follow its laws. They believed that the legitimate government was the one that was in place before the 1838 emigration.

Supporters of the Treaty Party were also against a united government, mostly because they did not favor John Ross as its leader. Under Watie's leadership, this faction continued to fight against Ross's followers. Conflict between the two factions often led to bloodshed. Although the new government warned against revenge killings, many Cherokee responded to violence with violence. Each conflicting faction blamed the other for cultivating aggression.

The Cherokee might have continued fighting for many more years had they not realized that it was putting their very survival at risk. Conflict within the Cherokee community made it difficult to defend against external threats. The Cherokee worried that one faction would again side with the US government or white communities against the other side. Both sides realized that there was strength in numbers. On August 6, 1846, the two sides—represented by Ross and Watie—signed a treaty recognizing the Cherokee Nation as one group.

Rebuilding a Society

Governance was just one problem among many for the Cherokee in Indian Territory. Families set about building log cabins and clearing the land for farms. Hunting, which the Cherokee had given up as part of the assimilation program in the East, once again became an important skill. There were few places to buy European-style clothes and shoes, so once again they relied on animal hide to make moccasins and breeches. Because the Cherokee had been forced to turn over their guns to army personnel, they used the bows and arrows, traps, and other weapons of their forefathers to catch game.

The Cherokee had been able to bring little with them over the Trail of Tears, and so they had to reconstruct almost everything from scratch. Kitchen utensils, especially, had often been left behind because they were heavy and took up a lot of room in the wagons. To fill their needs, older Cherokee relied on their pottery skills.

The land in Indian Territory was not as fertile as the land they had left behind. The government had promised to supply the Cherokee with food for a year after their arrival—until they had time to plant and harvest their first crops. However, there were problems with the private contractors the government hired to ration the supplies. Corrupt officials stole much of what was supposed to be given to the Native Americans, and contractors cut corners by buying cheap food. Sometimes the food was stored improperly, causing the meat to rot and the corn and flour to go moldy. Many people died of malnutrition and starvation because of corrupt agents who failed to fulfill their contracts and supply the Native Americans with basic necessities.

After moving west, the Cherokee built log cabins similar to this one instead of their traditional wattle and daub houses.

Sickness also continued to be a problem. Hundreds of Cherokee, weakened from their exhausting trip, caught illnesses such as smallpox, which was highly contagious. Many died soon after their arrival in Indian Territory. They did not have qualified doctors, and many of the traditional herbs and remedies that medicine men had used in the southeastern United States were not available in Oklahoma.

Despite these unfortunate beginnings, the Cherokee people survived—and thrived. In Indian Territory, the Cherokee soon rebuilt a democratic form of government, churches, schools, newspapers, and businesses. During what some historians call the Cherokee Golden Age, the new Cherokee capital, Tahlequah, and nearby Park Hill became centers of business and culture.

The Cherokee combined their ancient traditions with the most sensible parts of white society and built an educated, enlightened culture in the wilderness into which they were thrown. They built churches, divided their new country into voting districts, and wrote a new constitution. In 1844, the *Cherokee Advocate*, printed in both the Cherokee and English languages, became the first newspaper in Indian Territory. By the time of the Civil War, the Cherokee had built

HISTORY HAPPENED HERE: TAHLEQUAH, OKLAHOMA

Today, the capital of the Cherokee Nation is still Tahlequah, Oklahoma. Like other cities, Tahlequah offers shopping and dining. However, Tahlequah's cultural attractions are unique, as they focus on the history of the Cherokee Nation. They include a Cherokee Heritage Center, the John Ross Museum and Cemetery, and tours of important buildings such as the Cherokee National Capitol and Cherokee National Supreme Court Museum.

Shown here are young men playing a traditional Cherokee game called stickball during a parade in Tahlequah.

an entire school system. Their educational foundations rivaled those of white communities. In fact, many white settlements bordering the Cherokee Nation took advantage of the advanced school system and paid tuition to have their children attend the Cherokee schools.

Divided Again

The relative peace and prosperity of the Cherokee Nation would not last long. In 1861, the American Civil War broke out between the northern states (the Union) and the southern states (the Confederacy). Principal Chief John Ross asked the United States to send troops to protect its neutrality—as promised in the treaty—but this was yet another promise the United States failed to keep. The leaders of the Treaty Party sided with the Confederacy and convinced Ross to sign a formal alliance with the South. Other Cherokee fought on the side of the Union, pitting one faction of Cherokee against another. The Cherokee were heavily involved in the fighting that took place in and near Indian Territory. Though detailed records of Cherokee soldiers were not kept, historians have estimated that one-quarter of the Cherokee population was killed in the Civil War.

The Cherokee people lost more than lives as a result of the war. When the North emerged as victors, the Cherokee Nation was treated as a defeated enemy because it sided with the South. The United States used the Cherokee's alliance with the Confederates to punish them, taking huge chunks of the land that had been promised to them. Certain governmental powers were also taken away from the Cherokee Nation.

The Civil War was not the last time Cherokee land was threatened. As the United States continued to grow, old treaties were broken and new, unfair treaties were forced upon Cherokee leaders. The US government used its power to take land from the Cherokee Nation to make way for railroads needed to move people and goods to the new areas opening in the West.

The Indian Territory had been intended as a place where Native Americans could live separately from whites. However, whites soon moved to parts of the territory where Native Americans had not yet built homes, claiming the land for themselves. By 1880, more whites than natives lived in Indian Territory. In the late 1800s, what remained of Cherokee tribal land was divided into individual allotments and given to the Cherokee who were listed in the official census. Dishonest white speculators cheated many of these Cherokee out of their newly acquired land. The Cherokee people today live on less than one-third of 1 percent of the 7 million acres (2.8 million ha) originally granted to them by the Treaty of New Echota.

Most of the Cherokee Nation's government was officially dissolved in 1906, and Indian Territory was combined with Oklahoma

Territory to form the new state of Oklahoma. Against their wishes, the Cherokee became citizens of Oklahoma and the United States. At this time, it became the US government's job to appoint the Cherokee Nation's chief, taking away the Cherokee's right to even elect their own leader.

Still, the people fiercely clung to their identity as Native Americans and craved their independence. In 1971, a new Cherokee Nation emerged with the election of Principal Chief W. W. Keeler, the first democratically elected principal chief of the Nation since 1903. Since that time, the Cherokee people have struggled to obtain self-governance. They remind non-native Americans that they are more than capable of governing themselves. After all, they existed as an independent nation for thousands of years before the United States came into being.

Growing as a Nation

Despite their past hardships, the Cherokee have continued to grow as a people. They have become leaders in international business and industry. The Cherokee Nation established the first free, compulsory public school system in the United States, and Cherokee scholars have long been highly regarded by educational institutions around the world.

As of 2020, 573 federally recognized Native American tribes exist. Of those, three are made up of Cherokee: the Cherokee Nation, the United Keetoowah Band, and the Eastern Band. With more than 505,000 tribal citizens, the Cherokee Nation is the largest Native American tribe in the United States and Canada. More than 110,000 members of the Cherokee Nation live in northeastern Oklahoma, in 7,000 square miles (18,130 sq km) that were part of the area granted by the Treaty of New Echota. This land is not a reservation. It is an area recognized by the US federal government as a sovereign nation, controlled by Native American leaders.

Many of the thousands of Cherokee in the Eastern Band of Cherokee Indians in North Carolina are descended from those who avoided the Trail of Tears by escaping into the mountains or agreeing to exchange Cherokee citizenship for US citizenship. The United Keetoowah Band is mostly descended from the Old Settlers.

Today, they number more than 14,000, most of whom also live in Oklahoma. Each recognized tribe has its own government, though their makeup and relationship to the United States is similar, as they are all considered to be nations within the larger American country. Cherokee have certain rights within the United States and as citizens of the Cherokee tribes.

In addition to those who live on tribal lands, there are thousands of registered Cherokee living across the United States. Hundreds of thousands of people claim Cherokee heritage, including those who commute from tribal reservations and lands to their jobs in nearby cities across Oklahoma and North Carolina. Today, the Cherokee work and live alongside all other US citizens, often indistinguishable as a minority culture.

The Cherokee were once known as a "civilized tribe" that had adopted many customs and beliefs introduced to them by white settlers. Though they attempted to assimilate early, the Cherokee people have never lost hold of their heritage. In Cherokee, North Carolina, the Eastern Band of Cherokee hosts an annual Cherokee Indian Fair to showcase their remarkable culture and traditions. Traditional Cherokee also gather periodically at sacred ceremonial grounds, where they take part in a series of dances around the sacred fire. Some Cherokee perform these dances publicly as part of their effort to teach people about traditional Cherokee ways and beliefs. The Red Clay Council Grounds, the site of the last Cherokee council meetings before removal, was acquired by the state of Tennessee and is now a state park. The park includes a museum and outdoor replicas of a Cherokee council house from the 1830s, sleeping huts, and a farmstead.

Remembering the Past

The US government has acknowledged the Trail of Tears as a dark time in the country's history. The National Park Service established a path those on the Trail of Tears followed as a National Historic Trail that crosses nine US states: Alabama, Arkansas, Georgia, Illinois, Kentucky, Missouri, North Carolina, Oklahoma, and Tennessee. Along its length are memorials to those who died, museums, the forts built to shelter the Native Americans, and other sites at which

PAST MEETS PRESENT: RELIVING THE JOURNEY

On June 2, 2019, a group of cyclists from the Cherokee Nation and the Eastern Band of Cherokee set out on a three-week-long ride along a northern route of the Trail of Tears. The cyclists traveled from Georgia to Tahlequah, Oklahoma, a trip of about 950 miles (1,530 km). The Remember the Removal Bike Ride first began in 1984 as a way for young Cherokee to learn more about the history of their people. The 2019 riders continued this tradition, stopping along the trail at historic landmarks and gravesites that have been put up as historians have learned more about the Trail of Tears.

Journeys of remembrance are not limited to organized Cherokee activities; others have followed the trail on their own. In 1989, for example, Jerry Ellis, a Cherokee descendant, decided he would follow the path his ancestors took along the Trail of Tears. During the 1,000-mile (1,609 km) journey, he slept in a tent in the woods, fished in streams, and foraged in the woods for food. Ellis wrote about his journey in a book called *Walking the Trail: One Man's Journey along the Cherokee Trail of Tears.*

Many individuals have also sought to honor those who died along the trail. Early descendants returned to the Trail of Tears to mark the graves of their loved ones. Later descendants have visited points along the trail or followed it to honor the Cherokee who suffered on the journey.

Shown here is a group retracing the Trail of Tears in memory of those who made the original journey.

those traveling along the trail can learn about the history of the Trail of Tears. The Trail of Tears Association helps the National Park Service care for the historic trail and works to learn more about what happened on the trail through archaeological study. Some chapters of the association curate exhibits along the trail or provide signs for visitors to follow and learn more about what happened there.

Furthermore, individual states have dedicated land and resources to remember and build awareness about the Trail of Tears. Trail of Tears State Park in Missouri has an informative visitor center highlighting the history of the Trail of Tears, and Illinois named a state forest in remembrance of the trail. These modern tributes to the many who died along the Trail of Tears cannot change the past, but they promote hope about the relationship between the United States and Native Americans in the future.

The Cherokee have worked to ensure that their ancestors' struggle will never be forgotten. They have preserved diaries and letters written by those who traveled the Trail of Tears. Interviews with people who survived the journey were conducted to save their firsthand accounts of the tragic events. The Cherokee National Historical Society was formed in 1963 to do more work such as this to keep the history and culture of the Cherokee people safe.

The removal of the Cherokee people is an important part of Cherokee history and its collective memory. As Wilma Mankiller, a former principal chief of the Cherokee Nation, wrote, "Although it is so crucial for us to focus on the good things—our tenacity, our language and culture, the revitalization of tribal communities—it is also important that we never forget what happened to our people on the Trail of Tears. It was indeed our holocaust."[4]

How You See History

1. How do you think history would have been different if John Ross had never been elected?
2. Can you think of other historical events that bear a similarity to the Trail of Tears?
3. Why is it so important for everyone—not just Native Americans—to learn about the Trail of Tears?

1783
The Treaty of Paris ends the American Revolution. Because many Native Americans sided with the British, their lands are seen as a war prize by the United States government.

November 28, 1785
The Treaty of Hopewell defines the boundaries of Cherokee land. White Americans ignore these boundaries; instead of enforcing them, the government renegotiates the boundaries, causing the Cherokee to lose more land.

July 22, 1790
Congress passes the first Indian Trade and Intercourse Act, stating that only the federal government can negotiate treaties with Native Americans.

1803
The Louisiana Purchase opens up a huge area of land in the West. This area is seen as a good place to get Native Americans "out of the way" of white Americans.

1808
The first large group of Cherokee voluntarily relocates.

July 26, 1827
The Cherokee meet at New Echota to draft their first constitution and elect John Ross their principal chief.

1828
Andrew Jackson is elected president and is vocal about his opinion that removal is the best course of action for whites and Native Americans alike.

1829

Gold is found in modern-day Dahlonega, Georgia, causing a gold rush onto Cherokee lands.

May 28, 1830

Congress passes the Indian Removal Act.

March 3, 1832

The Supreme Court rules in *Worcester v. State of Georgia* that the state of Georgia cannot legally take land from the Cherokee. Andrew Jackson does not enforce the ruling.

December 29, 1835

A small group signs the Treaty of New Echota, which promises that the Cherokee will migrate west voluntarily in exchange for land and support from the US government. Most Cherokee oppose the treaty, but the federal government still enforces it.

June 6, 1838

The Trail of Tears begins as the US government sends in troops to force the reluctant Cherokee to migrate.

March 25, 1839

The Trail of Tears ends as the last group of Cherokee arrives in the West.

June 22, 1839

Major Ridge, John Ridge, and Elias Boudinot are assassinated for signing the Treaty of New Echota.

August 6, 1846

John Ross and Stand Watie sign a treaty recognizing the Cherokee Nation as one united group.

NOTES

Introduction: A History of Suffering

1. Elizabeth Prine Pauls, "Trail of Tears," *Encyclopedia Britannica*, modified November 11, 2019, www.britannica.com/event/Trail-of-Tears.
2. Quoted in Katie Marsico, *The Trail of Tears: The Tragedy of the American Indians* (Tarrytown, NY: Marshall Cavendish Benchmark, 2010), p. 57.
3. Russell Thornton, "Demography of the Trail of Tears Period: A New Estimate of Cherokee Population Losses," in William L. Anderson, ed., *Cherokee Removal: Before and After* (Athens, GA: University of Georgia Press, 1991), p. 93.

Chapter One: Life Before and During Colonization

1. Jerry Ellis, *Walking the Trail: One Man's Journey Along the Cherokee Trail of Tears* (New York, NY: Delacorte, 1991), p. iii.
2. Theda Perdue and Michael D. Green, *The Cherokee Removal: A Brief History with Documents* (Boston, MA: Bedford/St. Martin's, 2005), p. 3.
3. Quoted in Ken Martin, "1700 Through the Revolutionary War," History of the Cherokee, 1996, history-sites.com/cherokee/1700thro.html.
4. Quoted in William R. Reynolds Jr., *The Cherokee Struggle to Maintain Identity in the 17th and 18th Centuries* (Jefferson, NC: McFarland & Company, Inc., 2015), p. 271.
5. Joan Gilbert, *The Trail of Tears across Missouri* (Columbia, MO: University of Missouri Press, 1996), p. 6.

Chapter Two: Fighting for a Way of Life

1. Quoted in Seymour Dunbar, *A History of Travel in America* (Indianapolis, IN: Bobbs-Merrill Company, 1915), p. 557.
2. Quoted in "The Trail of Tears Across the Mississippi Valley," University of Vienna, accessed November 21, 2019, www.univie.ac.at/Anglistik/webprojects/LiveMiss/TrailofTears/trailparent.htm.
3. Quoted in "Andrew Jackson's Second Annual Message," PBS, accessed November 21, 2019, www.pbs.org/wgbh/aia/part4/4h3437t.html.
4. *Cherokee Nation v. Georgia*, 30 U.S. 1 (1831).

5. Quoted in Joan Gilbert, *The Trail of Tears across Missouri* (Columbia, MO: University of Missouri Press, 1996), p. 14.

Chapter Three: A Losing Battle

1. Quoted in Thurman Wilkins, *Cherokee Tragedy: The Ridge Family and the Decimation of a People* (Norman, OK: University of Oklahoma Press, 1986), p. 266.
2. Quoted in "Major Ridge," Georgia Tribe of Eastern Cherokee, accessed April 27, 2017. www.georgiatribeofeasterncherokee.com/MajorRidge.htm.
3. Quoted in Charles C. Royce, *The Cherokee Nation of Indians: A Narrative of Their Official Relations with the Colonial and Federal Governments* (Washington, DC: Smithsonian Institution—Bureau of Ethnology, 1887), p. 286.
4. Quoted in Donna Martinez, ed., *Documents of American Indian Removal* (Santa Barbara, CA: ABC-CLIO, 2019), p. 167.
5. Quoted in Joan Gilbert, *The Trail of Tears across Missouri* (Columbia, MO: University of Missouri Press, 1996), p. 32.
6. Quoted in Timothy D. Johnson, ed., *Memoirs of Lieut.-General Winfield Scott* (Knoxville, TN: University of Tennessee Press, 2015), p. 163.
7. Quoted in Russell Thornton, "Demography of the Trail of Tears Period: A New Estimate of Cherokee Population Losses," in William L. Anderson, ed., *Cherokee Removal: Before and After* (Athens, GA: University of Georgia Press, 1991), p. 79.
8. Quoted in Theda Purdue, "Cherokee Women and the Trail of Tears," in Karen Maschke, ed., *Women and the American Legal Order* (New York, NY: Routledge, 1997), p. 189.

Chapter Four: A Deadly Journey

1. "Two Accounts of the Trail of Tears: Wahnenauhi and Private John G. Burnett," Digital History, accessed November 23, 2019, www.digitalhistory.uh.edu/disp_textbook.cfm?smtID=3&psid=1147.
2. Quoted in Andrew Denson, *Monuments to Absence: Cherokee Removal and the Contest over Southern Memory* (Chapel Hill, NC: University of North Carolina Press, 2017), p. 34.

3. Quoted in "Saved the President's Life—Lived to Regret It," Georgia Tribe of Eastern Cherokee, accessed November 23, 2019, www.georgiatribeofeasterncherokee.com/Junaluska.htm.

4. "Trail of Tears," African American Policy Forum, accessed October 15, 2019, aapf.org/trail-of-tears.

Chapter Five: The Aftermath

1. Quoted in Thurman Wilkins, *Cherokee Tragedy: The Ridge Family and the Decimation of a People* (Norman, OK: University of Oklahoma Press, 1986), p. 332.

2. William G. McLoughlin, *After the Trail of Tears: The Cherokees' Struggle for Sovereignty 1839–1880* (Chapel Hill, NC: University of North Carolina Press, 1993), p. 16.

3. United States Office of Indian Affairs, *Annual Report of the Commissioner of Indian Affairs, 1839–1840* (Washington, DC: J. Gideon Jr., 1839), p. 69.

4. Wilma Mankiller and Michael Wallis, *Mankiller: A Chief and Her People* (New York, NY: St. Martin's Press, 1993), pp. 48–49.

FOR MORE INFORMATION

Books: Nonfiction

Behnke, Alison. *A Timeline History of the Trail of Tears*. Minneapolis, MN: Lerner Publishing Group, 2016.

Bowes, John P. *The Trail of Tears: Removal in the South*. New York, NY: Chelsea House, 2007.

King, Duane H. *The Cherokee Trail of Tears*. Portland, OR: Graphic Arts Center, 2008.

Schwartz, Heather E. *Forced Removal: Causes and Effects of the Trail of Tears*. North Mankato, MN: Capstone Press, 2015.

Books: Fiction

Bruchac, Joseph. *On This Long Journey: The Journal of Jesse Smoke, a Cherokee Boy, the Trail of Tears, 1838*. New York, NY: Scholastic Inc., 2014.

Foster, Sharon Ewell. *Abraham's Well*. New York, NY: Bethany House, 2006.

Websites

American Indian Removal

americanindian.si.edu/nk360/removal/index.cshtml

This interactive website includes maps, images, primary sources, and discussion questions.

American Native Press Archives, Sequoyah National Research Center

ualr.edu/Sequoyah

This website, which is part of the University of Arkansas–Little Rock, maintains a comprehensive collection of Native American newspapers, periodicals, and other publications; several pages are devoted to the Trail of Tears, providing a large selection of resources.

The Cherokee Nation

www.cherokee.org

The Cherokee Nation's internet library of information on the Trail of Tears includes primary source materials and firsthand accounts. The website also provides information on the culture and history of the Cherokee Nation before and after the Trail of Tears and on the government, population, events, and other aspects of Cherokee life today.

PBS LearningMedia: Trail of Tears

pbslearningmedia.org/resource/akh10.socst.ush.exp.trail/trail-of-tears

This video segment shows a reenactment of the Trail of Tears to give viewers a better understanding of this difficult journey.

Trail of Tears National Historic Trail

www.nps.gov/trte

This website provides information and stories about the routes the Native Americans took westward as well as the culture and history of various Native American groups today.

INDEX

PHOTO CREDITS

Cover National Geographic Image Collection/Alamy Stock Photo; pp. 4, 23, 30, 48 MPI/Getty Images; p. 6 Interim Archives/ Getty Images; p. 10 Transcendental Graphics/Getty Images; p. 12 RodClementPhotography/Shutterstock.com; p. 17 Burstein Collection/Corbis/VCG via Getty Images; p. 20 Charles Van Schaick/Wisconsin Historical Society/Getty Images; p. 22 duncan1890/DigitalVision Vectors/Getty Images; p. 28 Picturenow/Universal Images Group via Getty Images; p. 36 © iStockphoto.com/ZU_09; pp. 38, 53 Universal History Archive/ Universal Images Group via Getty Images; p. 41 Everett - Art/ Shutterstock.com; p. 45 Stock Montage/Getty Images; p. 55 Jeffrey M. Frank/Shutterstock.com; p. 57 Hum Historical/Alamy Stock Photo; p. 62 Bettmann/Bettmann/Getty Images; p. 66 Luke P Ferguson/Shutterstock.com; p. 69 Nikater/Wikimedia Commons; p. 72 Denver Post via Getty Images; p. 78 Danita Delimont/Alamy Stock Photo; p. 83 The History Collection/Alamy Stock Photo; p. 86 Apic/Getty Images; p. 87 Svineyard/Shutterstock.com; p. 91 Ed Lallo/The LIFE Images Collection via Getty Images/Getty Images.

ABOUT THE AUTHOR

Jennifer Lombardo earned her BA in English from the University at Buffalo and still resides in Buffalo, New York, with her cat, Chip. She has helped write a number of books for young adults, on topics ranging from world history to body image. In her spare time, she enjoys cross-stitching, hiking, and volunteering with Habitat for Humanity.